THE ENTERPRISE SHIELD: A GUIDE TO PREVENTING LEGAL BATTLES

SHIELDING YOUR BUSINESS: SAFEGUARDING YOUR BUSINESS AGAINST LAWSUITS AND CLASS ACTIONS

VENCE ATHANS

TABLE OF CONTENTS

INTRODUCTION

In today's business environment, finding your way through the many complexities of the legal system is akin to sailing through unpredictable and often treacherous waters. However, with the right knowledge and tools, companies can successfully navigate these challenges, regardless of size or industry. From costly lawsuits to damaging class actions, the potential for financial loss, reputational harm, and operational disruption is ever-present, but so is the potential for successful mitigation.

Consider the story of a small tech startup that, despite its innovative product and rapid growth, found itself entangled in a costly legal battle. A disgruntled former employee filed a lawsuit alleging wrongful termination and discrimination. The startup, unprepared for such an event, quickly found itself overwhelmed by legal fees, negative publicity, and a distracted management team. This legal storm nearly sank the promising company before it could establish itself fully.

Or take the case of a large multinational corporation that faced a massive class-action lawsuit due to a defective product. Despite having a sophisticated legal team, the company had overlooked critical quality-control measures. The resulting lawsuit not only led to a multi–million dollar settlement but also caused significant damage to the company's brand and consumer trust.

These stories are not isolated incidents but cautionary tales highlighting the importance of proactive legal risk management. Companies must be vigilant and prepared to face legal challenges head-on. This is not a task that can be deferred or taken lightly. It requires a strategic, comprehensive approach that permeates every level of the organization.

The Enterprise Shield: A Guide to Preventing Legal Battles is designed to be your guide and aims to provide you with the knowledge and tools necessary to anticipate potential legal threats, establish a strong legal framework, and implement effective risk-management strategies. It draws on real-world examples, best practices, and expert insights to equip you with actionable steps to protect your business.

We begin by exploring the various legal risks businesses commonly face and the tremendous impact litigation can have. From there, we dive into establishing a strong legal foundation through effective corporate governance, internal controls, and leveraging in-house and external legal counsel. We then move on to proactive risk management, focusing on regular risk assessments, appropriate insurance coverage, and strategic mitigation plans.

Subsequent chapters address specific areas of potential legal exposure, such as employment practices, product and service integrity, contract management, intellectual property protection, regulatory compliance, and crisis management. We emphasize the importance of learning from past legal challenges, as these experiences can provide valuable insights and build a culture of compliance and continuous improvement within your organization.

In an era when data protection and privacy are critical, we provide detailed guidance on understanding global data protection laws and implementing effective data security measures. Furthermore, we discuss the critical role of environmental and social responsibility in mitigating legal risks and building a strong, sustainable business.

Avoiding lawsuits and class actions is not merely about adhering to the letter of the law. It's about embedding a proactive and ethical approach into the heart of your organization. It's about creating a culture where compliance is not just a requirement but a core value; every organization member is committed to upholding these principles.

This book offers a comprehensive guide for businesses facing lawsuits and class actions. It emphasizes proactive measures, best practices, and effective risk management strategies. You will find the tools needed to minimize legal risks. The appendix includes self-assessment quizzes that promote a proactive approach to risk management. There are worksheets to help you with compliance check-ups, risk assessments, and identifying vulnerabilities. Additionally, you will find a clear overview of the legal processes in lawsuits and class actions. Each phase is explained, from initiation to resolution. This guide empowers you to safeguard your business against legal challenges.

By the end of this book, you will have a comprehensive understanding of how to shield your business from legal storms. You'll be equipped with the strategies and insights needed to navigate the complex legal landscape and build a resilient, successful organization. Let's embark on this journey together and ensure your business survives and thrives in the face of legal challenges.

UNDERSTANDING LEGAL RISKS

In today's world, every business owner needs to understand the intricacies of legal risks deeply. It doesn't matter whether you've just entered the business world or you're a veteran in maneuvering around the business environment; understanding the delicate nature of legal risks is a big step to overcoming setbacks in your business and entering into the arena of success and fulfillment. So, in this chapter, I will introduce you to each potential legal threat you can face in your business. Also, I'll teach you how these risks cut across various aspects of operations and how they can affect decision-making. Once you understand these hidden gimmicks, you can fortify yourself with the knowledge you need to prevent possible liabilities for your business. Let's get right into it!

EMPLOYMENT PRACTICES

For any business to survive or thrive well, the employees have a huge role to play, and that's why employment practices are one of the significant risks that companies must handle with care. Such challenges can arise from discrimination, harassment, wrongful termination, or salary disputes, which can make or break any business. A number of advocates or social groups are fighting for workers' rights; the result of their fights is that companies must treat their workers fairly. The side effects of failing to do so are frequently unpleasant—they can range from expensive lawsuits to affecting the smooth running of your business and even tarnishing your business's image. Let's look at various employment practices next.

Discrimination

Discrimination within a workplace can significantly threaten its stability. Without proper management, it can lead to the loss of committed employees, expensive legal battles, and lasting damage to the company's reputation. Despite societal advancements and full knowledge of anti-discrimination laws, various organizations exhibit bias in their hiring processes, promotions, and workplace interactions.

Discrimination arises from prejudices directed at specific demographic groups based on race, age, beliefs, or gender, though it encompasses a broader range of biases. Numerous laws, including the Civil Rights Act, prohibit unlawful employment practices. When a company faces a lawsuit, the repercussions can be severe. If such cases gain media traction, the organization's public image may suffer, jeopardizing customer relationships. Furthermore, companies with a reputation for discriminatory practices may experience decreased productivity and diminished employee motivation, ultimately compromising their long-term success.

Harassment

If you run a business where employees frequently experience harassment, you need to address the issue promptly to mitigate potential legal risks. Laws regarding workplace harassment are stringent and clearly define harassment as unacceptable behavior.

Harassment can manifest as threats, discrimination, or sexual advances, creating a toxic work environment that hampers employee productivity. In addition to the risk of legal action, businesses may face severe public backlash, which can significantly hinder their growth and reputation.

Wrongful Termination

Wrongful termination, just as the name implies, is when an employee is unjustly laid off from their job, and in the process, there's a breach of federal laws or the company's standards. Wrongful termination can occur as a form of retaliation, a contract violation, or other company policies.

For instance, if a company wrongfully terminates an employee simply due to bias in age, gender, or race, such a business can incur costly proceedings. Also, a business owner can decide to dismiss their employees simply because they participated in any form of legal activity, and once this happens, such businesses can face huge penalties.

PRODUCT LIABILITY

Now, let's look at another legal risk: product liability. It's a legal entitlement for a business to produce or sell destructive and harmful products. If you ask any manufacturer or distributor about their biggest fear in regard to their business, 8 out of 10 will likely mention product liability. What's the cause of this fear? Harmful or defective products can affect consumers negatively, resulting in expensive lawsuits and causing defamation to their business.

Product liability is divided into three sections:

- **Design flaw:** This is a deformity or flaw in a product's design that can harm the product. Even if the intention of the product was to be made right, such intentions become useless.
- **Manufacturing flaw:** In this case, the product has a proper design, but a single error during the production process can make the product flawed.
- **Refusal to warn:** Normally, every business owner should release a public notice to their consumers about the risks associated with their products. So, if the business owner has not done this, it can lead to lawsuits.

Talking about product liability, it's not only manufacturers that are susceptible to this. Product liability claims can affect everyone involved in the distribution chain.

CONTRACT DISPUTES

Once a business understands the concept of business litigation, it can improve its operations and legal procedures. Often, these disputes can result from misinterpretations, refusal to fulfill responsibilities, or disagreements over the contract terms.

It doesn't matter whether a quarrel occurs due to an employment contract, real estate contract, or any other contract; you must handle everything appropriately because, in the end, if it's not adequately handled, it can impair the virtue of your business.

So, what exactly is a contract dispute?

A contract dispute is a disparity between two groups regarding the conditions or performance of a legal contract, such as a master service agreement. Contract disputes occur when one group thinks that the other group has refused to fulfill their duties, and in the end, it leads to disagreements that may require a legal settlement.

The concept of a contract dispute depends on whether the contract violation is material or minor.

When discussing a material breach of contract, it has a consequential effect on the contract's main aim and can result in legal actions or a contract ending. Even though a minor breach is a form of breach, it doesn't subvert the whole contract and can result in minor consequences. However, when there's a clear, accurate, and adequately understood term, it can avert disagreements that lead to disputes.

How Do Contract Disputes Occur?

Contract disputes can occur for several reasons. Let's look at some of the general ones.

Negligence of Obligation

A prevalent cause of contract disputes is when a particular group refuses to fulfill its obligations. It can be in the form of not paying wages when due, failing to confirm the required standards, or failing to deliver a service promptly.

Misconstruction of Contract

The two parties involved may not have a proper understanding of what the contract is all about. So, imagine the first party is carrying out the contract based on what they understand about the agreement, which is different from what the second party understands. This can lead to disputes.

Changes in Conditions

When unavoidable circumstances like changes in market conditions or unexpected events occur, it can affect the ability of a group to meet up with their end of the contract, causing quarrels.

Types of Contract Disputes

We have several contract disputes, but I'd like to introduce you to the three general ones. And what are they?

- **Business contract disputes:** This type of dispute arises from inappropriate product or service delivery, when confidential agreements are breached, or even unmet payment conditions.
- **Real estate contract disputes:** Real estate disputes occur when property flaws, infractions of sake conditions, or a breach in lease agreements arise.
- **Employment agreement disputes:** This last one is altercations over employment conditions, wages or workplace benefits, inappropriate termination, or misconduct in the workplace.

INTELLECTUAL PROPERTY

Intellectual property (IP) is another legal risk associated with possible threats regarding an organization's IP, trademarks, copyrights, and trade secrets. The value of an IP is relatively high, so a business must avert risks by putting in place measures to safeguard against violations. These measures establish strategies to ensure the accurate management of the organization's IP, prevent possible legal quarrels, and put in place reservation plans for potential risks.

Let's look at the definitions of intellectual property risks.

Intellectual property risks are the possible threats or dangers associated with a company's IP, consisting of patents, trademarks, or copyrights. These threats can occur from different sources, resulting in substantial monetary loss, business image damage, and contention disadvantages.

So, what exactly are the types of intellectual property risks?

- **Infringement:** Infringement can happen when a company uses another company's property that has undergone a patent or copyright. However, this act is not always deliberate and can result in expensive legal lawsuits.
- **Theft:** This is when an illegal party steals or uses a company's IP without reaching out to them, which can cause a decrease in revenue for such a company.
- **Inadequate protection:** A company might be negligent in protecting its IP, allowing other illegal parties to duplicate its product or services. In the end, the company may lose its market share.
- **Nonadherence:** A company failing to obey IP laws and regulations can lead to legal penalties or even affect business relationships.
- **Tech transfer threats:** These involve threats that come with transferring technology from one organization to another—for instance, sharing your IP with an organization that can become a possible threat or losing its edge over the IP.

REGULATORY COMPLIANCE

Regulatory compliance is simply adhering to the rules and regulations of the government and other regulatory agencies. The rules are in several forms, including laws, regulations, standards, and policies. The main objective of regulatory compliance is to ensure that organizations operate correctly according to the usual standard. It can be done through environmental laws, financial regulations, and data protection. Regulatory compliance can be tricky; the precise requirements differ, which hinge significantly on the business and its location. However, in the end, regulatory compliance is essential for any business.

How Regulatory Risks Come to Play in Businesses

Regulatory risks arise from the fact that changes in rules and regulations can negatively affect businesses. These modifications can occur from different regulatory bodies and impact businesses in many ways. Let's have a closer look at how regulatory risks come to be:

- **Shifting rules and regulations:** The government's rules and regulations are flexible and often change. Occasionally, these changes can affect businesses because they increase compliance costs, and in the end, such companies have no other option but to adapt their system or services. For example, companies are forced to upgrade their equipment when stringent environmental regulations are enforced.
- **Changes in public opinion:** Public protest over the mode of operations in an industry can result in new rules. For instance, if there's a public uproar because of the inappropriate data privacy system in a particular

organization, the government might decide to enforce tightened rules on data protection. Ultimately, companies have no option but to change their data collection methods.

- **Doubt and delay:** Before a new rule can be enforced, it doesn't just happen in the twinkle of an eye; it takes more time than expected. Therefore, this lack of assurance can leave businesses unable to plan and even halt or disrupt big company projects.

Importance of Adherence to Legal Laws in Mitigating Risk

- **Prevents legal liabilities:** When a company chooses not to adhere to laws and regulations, it can lead to legal actions and punishments, and in the end, it can have a significant impact on the company's finances. So, companies can reduce the potential for legal disputes and heavy financial requirements by obeying legal rules and regulations.
- **Protects the business's image:** In today's technology age, every business owner should be conscious of protecting their reputation, which can spread across the internet almost instantly. The adverse effects that noncompliance to rules can bring are not worth the stress. Just like when you want to build a house, it can take years before you finally finish building, but you can demolish your home in just one day. That's the same way it is with the reputation of your business. Just one single flaw can bring your business down in a minute.
- **Have a competitive edge:** Several companies have fierce competitors that are doing well business-wise. So, adhering strictly to the rules can give your company a competitive edge.

Understanding legal risks goes beyond mere compliance; a strategic imperative safeguards a company's reputation and fosters its success. By effectively identifying, assessing, and mitigating these risks, you establish a framework to thwart expensive litigation and position your business as a leader within its sector. Moreover, with this knowledge, you can understand the laws and run your business right, despite the complexities of the legal system. With this foundation in place, let's proceed to the next chapter, where we will explore strategies for building a robust legal framework for your business.

ESTABLISHING A SOLID LEGAL FRAMEWORK

By default, business owners are big dreamers who love envisioning new ways to do things. The challenge is that they paint the big picture before setting up the business's mechanics. Most founders view the legal setup of their business as a time-consuming chore that is set aside until it becomes a pressing necessity. But the truth is, in order to ensure the health and sustainability of your business the legal framework should be prioritized and considered, even before bringing other people on board or pitching investors.

The legal structure of your business ensures that you are operating legally and that your products and services are protected from loss, which is significant when things change in your team. A notable example is the Winklevoss twins, who failed to legally document the early stages of their social media platform, which allowed Mark Zuckerberg to launch Facebook using part of the code he wrote (Janeczko, 2020).

Although they can be easily avoided, legal problems are among the top reasons many startups fail. Founders who need to identify their business's legal demands will realize a problem later in the journey. Specific structures discussed in this chapter must be present to ensure that your business is duly protected.

CORPORATE GOVERNANCE

Generally, governance ensures that everyone within an organization follows a straightforward and appropriate decision-making process that controls the company. In a business context, it refers to rules, practices, and procedures by which a company is governed. Corporate governance exists to build an environment of transparency, trust, and accountability necessary for financial stability and business growth. Here are the three standard models that govern businesses:

Board of Directors

The board of directors is a collection of individuals operating as a group to fulfill the defined roles within a business organization. This board must hire the CEO or manager of the business, who recruits all the other employees.

However, the board of directors as a corporate governing body has evolved regarding a business's culture and values, as it is always comfortable and practical for most people to function as a group. This gave rise to several governance models of how a board of directors can function and the four standard models from which a business can choose.

- **Manage focus:** In this model, the manager governs the board, acting as a "rubber stamp" for the CEO. The board functions as an advisory board and reacts only to the manager's ideas. In most cases, this is not a recommended model for a value-added business (Boland, 2021).

- **Proactive board:** This kind of board speaks as one voice and usually has a proactive manager who speaks for the organization as a group. It can work well because the manager and the board are on the same level in decision-making, and it is best to take advantage of emerging opportunities.
- **Geographic representation:** This model prioritizes the investors the board members represent, found in large boards typically consisting of 24–50 individuals. The board members are obligated to represent the interests of individuals in a particular geographic location.
- **Community representation:** In this case, the board members represent the community rather than the organization. An example of this kind of board is the one found in schools, where the members are elected to represent the interests of the parents.

Responsibilities of the Board of Directors

Each board has its own way of handling the activities of the organization, but its five significant responsibilities include:

- **Recruit, evaluate, retain, supervise, and compensate the manager.** Value-added business boards need to intentionally look for the best candidate for the position of Managing Director. The importance of this position is why recruiting, supervising, evaluating, and compensating the CEO is the most critical function of the board of directors. The active search for a candidate within an industry will help identify competent people for the position.

- **Guide the business on the right path.** The board is responsible for mapping out the business's vision, mission, and goals in conjunction with the general manager. This, in turn, directs the organization on what it needs to achieve.

- **Govern the organization and relationship with the manager.** An organization's governance system involves how the board interacts with the general manager, and it is the responsibility of the members to develop it. The CEO and the board of directors interact at intervals, usually in meetings held periodically. Although most boards have switched to holding meetings four or eight times a year, it is a monthly meeting. Everything that happens in the interim between these meetings is conveyed to the board through video conferences or emails.

- **Establish a policy-based governance system.** The governance template provides the framework, but the board is responsible for developing policies. In other words, the board develops policies to guide the actions of the manager and its members; thus, the rules should be policy-based.

- **Fiduciary responsibility to business assets and member investments.** The welfare of investors and the integrity of company resources hinge on the fiduciary responsibilities shouldered by the board of directors. Thus, the board must safeguard the company's assets, including its properties, facilities, equipment, and human resources.

Compliance Programs

Corporate governance programs are rules, policies, guidelines, and practices that a company establishes internally to ensure its employees comply with laws, regulations, and industrial standards (PittLaw, 2023). These programs help promote ethical conduct, protect the public's perception, mitigate risk, and promote the company's reputation by ensuring it complies with national and international law. They are also crucial for organizations of all sizes to prevent unethical, illegal, or inappropriate employee behavior.

However, to create a program that can adequately prevent legal violations, detect misconduct, and address issues promptly, the documented policies and procedures of the company must spell out the business expectations on compliance with relevant regulations and ethical behaviors. Also, employee training programs should be organized to provide all employees with awareness of your business's procedures and policies.

Moreover, a check-and-balance system must be in place to monitor the activities within the company and ensure that all key players are alerted of potential compliance concerns, which includes internal investigations and regular audits. There should also be a medium where employees and stakeholders can address their concerns, including avenues for anonymously reporting violations.

Implementing a Compliance Program

Developing and implementing a corporate compliance program is crucial because several frameworks depend on your business and the current state of this program. Below are the steps that can help you achieve a compliance program setup:

- **Conduct a thorough risk assessment.** Start by accessing and identifying the compliance risk specific to your jurisdiction and business. Examine areas of potential vulnerability and prioritize them based on the impact of noncompliance.
- **Develop your policies.** Document all the procedures and policies you have in place and develop any that do not exist. Ensure your policies are clear and accessible and address the risks identified in the first step.
- **Train the employees.** It is crucial to provide awareness and regular training programs to educate your employees about the company's policies and obligations to comply.
- **Monitor compliance.** Establish a thorough monitoring system to assess compliance with policies and procedures. Conduct internal reviews and monitor key performances to address potential compliance issues promptly. Auditors should look out for new regulations that have gone into effect and ensure that the company policies are up-to-date.
- **Establish an investigating process.** A secure and confidential reporting system should be implemented so all employees can file complaints. This step requires that you write out the procedure for investigating noncompliance claims. Individual players and groups should be held accountable, as this is effective for maintaining a healthy compliance program.

Internal Controls: Auditing

From planning to reporting your business's financial procedures, the auditing process ensures that your financial statements are accurate, helping to build trust among your stakeholders. The overall concept of auditing explores the systematic examination of a company's financial records conducted by independent professionals known as auditors. This process involves evaluating the accuracy of financial information, identifying a potential error, and ensuring compliance with the applicable law.

Auditing is essential in providing credibility to financial information and holding corporate entities accountable. It follows a systematic approach governed by a group of generally accepted auditing standards (GAAS) to enhance reliability and consistency. It involves a thorough review of the business financial records, internal controls, and management practices to provide input on the accuracy of financial reporting.

Importance of Auditing in Business

The vital roles that auditing plays in businesses include:

- Boosting the confidence of external stakeholders like investors and creditors by providing an independent assessment of financial records
- Facilitating investment decisions and market efficiency
- Identifying areas for improvement and addressing loopholes in internal controls
- Serving as an ideal deterrent to fraudulent activities and misconduct
- Promoting ethical behaviors and protecting the interests of stakeholders
- Providing valuable feedback to businesses by providing insights into financial health

The Initial Phase of the Auditing Process: Audit Planning

Auditing financial records begins with detailed planning, including gathering relevant information, setting objectives, and developing an auditing strategy to guide auditors' work. Identifying the audit scope is an essential step in audit planning; the auditor is charged with marking out specific areas to be audited, such as internal controls, financial records, or compliance with regulations. The scope will lie in the auditor's understanding of the organization, its industry, and the specific concerns that must be addressed (Datasniper, 2024).

Risk assessment is another process considered in audit planning. It evaluates existing and potential risks affecting the business's financial statement. Auditors can use various techniques, such as interviews, inquiries, and analytical procedures, to understand the company's risk profile, which will help them plan the audit procedures.

Moreover, auditors can craft an auditing strategy tailored to the business's needs based on the company's risk assessment results to ensure smooth audit execution.

The Execution Phase: Conducting the Audit

Once the planning phase is finished, the next stage is ushered in, at which time auditors gather evidence and test internal controls to validate the accuracy of the company's financial records. This phase comprises:

- **Gathering and analyzing evidence:** Auditors can use various methods, including observation, examination of documents, and confirmation with third parties, to support their conclusions.
- **Testing internal controls:** Internal controls are policies and protocols established by a company to ensure the reliability of financial reports. They are a significant aspect of the auditing process because they test the effectiveness of these controls to ascertain the level of risk associated with the financial statement.

- **Audit sampling:** Due to the volume of transactions and limited resources, auditors use various sampling techniques to obtain meaningful and reliable results. The methods used include statistical or judgmental sampling, depending on the situation.

The Last Phase of the Audit Process: Audit Reporting

The final phase of the process involves concluding the audit report and communicating the findings to the company's management and stakeholders. Audit reporting begins with preparing the audit report itself. This process presents the result of the audit process in a deliverable format, typically including an introduction, a description of the scope and objective of the audit, a conclusion of findings, and the auditor's comments.

Once an audit report is finalized, the auditors communicate their findings to management and stakeholders by discussing crucial aspects of their findings and making recommendations for improvement.

LEGAL COUNSEL

As your business grows, the complexities of acquisition, personnel, contracts, and finances grow as well. These matters can take up the manager's time, which could be better served with other tasks. Having either in-house or external counsel manage the legal aspect of your business will surely boost the productivity of the administrative part of the business.

Benefits of In-House Legal Counsel

1. **Help streamline the organization's focus:** Running a business puts you in a position where every matter pulls you in, particularly with legally related issues. You may have to manage some relationships with a private attorney to keep up with the legal demands of the business. However, in-house counsel can effectively manage the legal matters of your business, such as legal expenditures, which in turn add valuable time to business owners.

2. **Have your best interest at heart:** An in-house legal counsel can act proactively to identify future legal challenges by dedicating all their time and interest to your business. Identifying individuals with the right skills and experience will prepare your business for legal demands.

3. **Peace of mind:** Having individuals oversee your business's legal matters and dedicating 100% of their time to it can reduce the stress of anticipating future challenges

4. **Add strategic value:** Adding in-house counsel to your team will help your business make strategic decisions to prevent unnecessary risks and liabilities.

5. **There is always a solution:** In-house counsel operates and makes decisions with the company in mind. They help business colleagues find solutions to problems rather than shutting an idea down because it will not work.

Selecting and Managing External Legal Advisors

External counsel refers to lawyers a business hires from outside the organization. They help companies of all sizes support in-house counsel by resolving issues beyond their jurisdiction or replacing them entirely.

External counsel is handy for businesses that want to refrain from investing in full-time in-house counsel. Equally, they are helpful for startups where a generalist lawyer is needed in a team with specialist skills like litigation. They assist individuals and businesses in providing valuable legal advice, representation, and support when needed. Nevertheless, how can a company manage an external counsel?

Here are some top tips that may be useful:

- Choose external counsel with expertise in specific areas of law relevant to your company's legal needs. Check their portfolio, references, and reputation to ensure they suit your requirements.
- Establish a clear guideline to manage expectations from each vendor, which will give both parties an avenue to provide value for the business. The guideline should cover billing hygiene, what gets charged, commercial terms, and charges for billable tasks.
- Split your priorities into impact and importance to determine which legal matters stay with in-house counsel and which move to external counsel. Prioritization allows businesses to address critical legal needs and allocate resources effectively.
- Your business needs to track the results of external counsel to assess the efficiency of current systems and processes and note improvements.
- Technology can enhance efficiency through collaboration tools, document management systems, and information sharing. It can also help manage external counsel through contract automation.

- Build a collaborative working relationship with your external counsel by sharing insights and information about your business to help them understand its needs.

A system that oversees your company's matters, such as compliance programs and legal counsel, may be crucial in addressing your business's legal concerns. However, proactive risk management measures will help you level up. The next chapter will explore risk assessment techniques and the best insurance system for covering your business against loss.

PROACTIVE RISK MANAGEMENT

Whether you're moving to an exciting new city, throwing a discus, or leading a thriving business, one thing is crystal clear: you're taking risks! Every decision you make—running a cozy outlet or managing a vast business empire—requires you to weigh the pros and cons carefully. The reality of potential challenges, from launching a game-changing product to expanding your operations, highlights the urgent need for effective, proactive risk management. Unlike reactive strategies, this forward-thinking approach is all about anticipating and preparing for risks before they even appear on the horizon. It's a vital game plan for successful business endeavors. So, how do you navigate these risks wisely? In this chapter, get ready to explore the frameworks that will break down the complexities of risk management and empower you to take charge!

RISK ASSESSMENT

Risk assessment is a practical and crucial process that involves identifying potential threats, determining the probability of risk occurrence, and deciding the steps to be implemented to eliminate or control such risks. When applied diligently, this process allows you a sense of control and confidence in your decision-making, as well as empowers you to run your business despite the uncertainties that come with it.

Identifying Risks

The initial step is to pinpoint the issue to address a challenge effectively. Identifying risks is an essential proactive measure that entails recognizing and evaluating current and potential hazards to an organization, its operations, and its workforce. This forward-thinking strategy equips you to handle unexpected situations, creating a mindset of preparedness and foresight.

Business risks come in a variety of forms, but they can be divided into four main categories:

Strategic Risk

Strategy is one of the most significant parts of every business, and a wrong or failed strategy can greatly weaken a business. For example, if a new product does not sell well, there is a significant risk of such a business running at a loss. Other examples of strategic risks include entering a new market without sufficient research or over-relying on a single supplier or customer.

Internal risks fall under this category; these are risks that ensue due to decisions taken by a company's managerial team. These decisions can create physical or tangible risks. On-site risks such as fire outbreaks, equipment malfunctions, or using hazardous materials in manufacturing processes can jeopardize production, endanger employees, and lead to legal or financial penalties.

The recent demise of Silicon Valley Bank, one of the largest financial institutions in the United States, highlights the perilous consequences of ineffective strategic choices. Known for its focus on lending to technology firms, the bank neglected to diversify its portfolio and concentrated solely on issuing loans. This narrow approach quickly led to substantial financial setbacks, exacerbated by the Federal Reserve's hike in interest rates. Efforts to restore the bank's fiscal health proved unsuccessful, prompting a significant exodus of clients who withdrew their funds en masse. During this withdrawal frenzy, the bank liquidated assets, including devalued bonds resulting from rising interest rates, incurring a staggering loss of $1.8 billion. Boasting assets totaling $212 billion in 2022, the bank collapsed in March 2023, marking the second-largest failure in American history (Forbes, 2023).

Another typical example of a failed business strategy is that of one-time photography giant Kodak. It used to be the world's biggest film company but focused on film production and failed to keep up with the digital revolution. In 2001, Kodak acquired a photo-sharing site called Ofoto. However, instead of pioneering what might have been the predecessor of Instagram, Kodak used Ofoto to try to get more people to print digital images. This strategic misstep and the failure to develop digital cameras for the mass market for fear of eradicating its all-important film business led to its downfall. Competitors like the Japanese firm Canon grasped this opportunity and outlived the giant (Brand Minds, 2018).

Operational Risk

Operational risks can be internal, external, or a combination of both. External operational risks include natural disasters that damage physical premises or equipment, pandemics that force people to shelter in place or work from home, or a server outage that causes technical problems like lack of power or disrupted internet connectivity. Internal business risks are often related to human error or misconduct, such as data breaches, cyberattacks, identity theft, embezzlement, money laundering, criminal records, and intellectual property theft.

Malfunctioning machinery or operational processes also fall under internal business risks. For instance, if a business process fails or a particular machinery stops functioning, the business will not be able to produce any goods/products. As a result, the business cannot sell the products and make money. If this risk is not addressed in time, it can lead to the eventual closure of such businesses.

Enron is an ideal case study of how operational risks can ruin a company. Enron was once considered a giant in the energy sector due to its innovation and rapid growth. However, deep management and corporate governance issues lay beneath the surface. The executive team engaged in unethical practices and made risky decisions, ultimately leading to the company's downfall. For instance, they used accounting loopholes to hide debts, which misled investors and inflated the company's stock prices. This kind of misconduct showcases how operational risk can stem from leadership decisions. In addition to misconduct, failed merger projects played a significant role in Enron's failure. The company attempted to expand through mergers that did not pan out as planned. These failed projects drained financial resources and damaged the company's reputation. In 2001, Enron experienced one of the biggest business failures in American history due to managerial misconduct, failed merger project management, and corporate governance issues (BBC, 2021).

Reputational Risk

Reputational risk is a critical type of business risk that can have a lasting and profound effect on a company, even after its resolution. If the image of a company is tarnished in the market, there is a high chance of such a company losing its customer base. This risk can be triggered by various factors, including faulty products or services, poor customer support experiences, adverse publicity about a company's staff, or high-profile failures in the press. Failure to address business risks is also a reputational risk. Security breaches, fraud incidents, noncompliance with laws and regulations, and poor financial performance all damage a business's reputation, often with severe and long-lasting consequences.

The 2015 Volkswagen scandal is an excellent example of this risk's danger. The automobile company was found to have installed software in 11 million diesel engines worldwide that cheated on emissions tests. This scandal led to a significant decrease in sales and plummeting stock prices, which had far-reaching legal and financial implications. The cost to fix the affected cars, combined with the fines and legal settlements, ran into tens of billions of dollars. The scandal left an indelible mark on the Volkswagen brand, demonstrating the far-reaching implications of reputational risk (BBC, 2015).

Compliance Risk

A business must adhere to established guidelines and legal requirements to operate successfully. When a company fails to comply with such standards, it significantly diminishes its chances of sustainability in the long run. It is best to check the legal and environmental practices before forming a business entity. Otherwise, the business will face unprecedented challenges and unnecessary lawsuits in the future. Laws related to occupational health and safety, equipment certification requirements, cybersecurity, taxes, and more are constantly being updated, and claiming ignorance of these changes is not a valid defense.

In 2019, Facebook (now Meta) was fined $5 billion by the Federal Trade Commission (FTC) for privacy violations after the Cambridge Analytics scandal. This penalty resulted from Facebook's lax privacy practices, which allowed third parties like Cambridge Analytics to access the personal information of millions of its users without explicit consent. Not only did Facebook incur a substantial financial loss, but it also had to make significant changes to its operations to comply with new privacy standards. Furthermore, these changes affected Facebook's ability to target ads as accurately as before, affecting its revenue streams (Cooling, 2024).

Prioritizing Risks

Once your risks have been determined, you should develop a preference scale to evaluate current and future threats using the following factors:

Risk Severity

This refers to the level to which a risk can cause damage to an organization. Using severity, a risk matrix can be created to identify the most severe risks and those that would cause negligible damage to the company. A risk matrix is a tool that helps you visualize and prioritize risks based on their severity and likelihood of occurrence. By plotting risks on a matrix, you can identify the most critical risks that need immediate attention and those that can be managed with existing resources. This will help to determine the risks that should be addressed first.

Risk Manageability

This refers to the overall ability of a company to manage risk, whether the company can handle an occurrence of the risk, and its overall impact. A more manageable risk would have a negligible business impact if it occurred, whereas a less manageable risk could disrupt business operations.

Resource Availability

This factor is based on the resources available to the managerial team for assuaging risk. This includes personnel, time, cost, and other resources needed for effective remediation.

Cost

This factor places the monetary value of risk into consideration for prioritization. Based on the cost of a certain risk, the executive team of an industry may choose to prioritize a more costly risk over risk with less monetary value at stake.

Risk Sensitivity

This is a quantitative risk-assessment tool that helps determine how changes in risk affect the overall risk posture and the affected company, consequently helping you choose a mitigation strategy. A more sensitive risk should be given more attention than less sensitive one.

The primary strategy in grading risks is to assess their likelihood and impact. Likelihood refers to how probable it is that a risk will occur, while impact refers to how significant the consequences will be if it does. The higher the probability and impact of a risk, the more attention and resources it deserves. Organizing risks through regulatory and legal penalties is another line of action. Some businesses may pay a fine to avoid dealing with a risk, which allows them to prioritize based on the potential fine.

MITIGATION STRATEGIES

Mitigation involves developing and implementing plans to eliminate or lessen the impact of identified risks. Risk mitigation is essential for maintaining a business's existence, reputation, safety, and profitability. A company that can proactively manage its risks can be sure to have its assets and stakeholders protected and have fewer cases of disruptions. These management strategies include:

Business Continuity Planning

This is the most common risk-response strategy organizations use to manage risks. This strategy aims to identify significant risks to the organization and make plans for what the organization will do to lessen or eliminate those risks.

Contingency Planning

This includes specific actions that a company's executive team must take if a risk arises. Depending on the risk, the contingency plan might consist of extra funding or the employment of additional staff to respond to the risk.

Risk Review

A risk review is a periodic evaluation of the effectiveness and efficiency of the risk-management process. It involves checking whether the risks are still relevant and accurate and whether the risk responses are still appropriate and sufficient. The risk review can help a company identify new or emerging risks, adjust risk priorities and rankings, and improve risk-management practices.

INSURANCE

Picture being the managing director of one of the most promising accounting firms in the state, with many distinguished people in your clientele; your business seems to be going well until your firm gets sued for incorrect tax advice. Unfortunately, your company is uninsured and is on the verge of incurring massive financial losses due to legal settlement fees.

Insurance is the bulletproof vest that every business requires, and it is vital to understand what type of insurance your company needs and how to use it.

Types of Insurance Coverage

Insurance has a lot of coverage packages to offer; we will review some of them next.

General Liability Insurance

It provides coverage against claims that may arise when a third party is injured on an organization's premises. This insurance accounts for third-party bodily injury when a customer falls and gets hurt inside the company. It also covers third-party property damage, like when an employee accidentally damages the floor while installing equipment at a customer's home. Additionally, it protects against reputational harm, including libel, slander, and violations of a competitor's privacy. Advertising injury, such as copyright infringement and false claims, is also covered. The insurance company can also handle lawsuit settlements. However, it does not cover damage to business property, mistakes in professional services, or work-related injuries or illnesses.

Professional Liability Insurance

It is a form of business liability insurance that protects against claims of mistakes in professional services. This insurance covers costs associated with these claims, including legal fees, court judgments, settlements, and even penalties from licensing boards. However, it does not cover provisions for bodily injury, property damage, data breaches, violations of employee rights, or illnesses and injuries.

For example, if a client claims that your services have caused them financial losses, this insurance will cover legal fees, settlements, and judgments up to the policy's limits. Professional liability insurance is essential for businesses that offer professional services, such as architects, accountants, information technology professionals, engineers, and real estate agents.

Directors and Officers (D&O) Property Damage or Company Disputes

Director's and officer's liability insurance covers defense costs, settlements, and other expenses for lawsuits or claims against directors or officers. This insurance arises from allegations that a director or officer has breached their fiduciary responsibility while serving the company.

Lawsuits against executive directors and officers are becoming more common. Without D&O insurance, both the company's assets and the personal assets of directors and officers are at risk.

D&O insurance helps protect company leaders if they are accused of causing financial harm, breaking workplace laws, treating employees unfairly, making false statements, or violating copyright. However, it does not cover physical injuries, property damage, or company disputes.

Selecting Insurance Policies

Business insurance is an essential safety net. When sued by a client or when the need to shut down certain operations arises, insurance can help cover those unexpected costs. However, picking the right coverage and policies can be challenging. How do you determine the type of insurance your business needs?

The right insurance for your business depends on your business needs and the laws in your state and industry.

Steps Involved in Choosing an Insurance Policy

Choosing an insurance policy can feel overwhelming for business owners. However, breaking it down into clear steps can make the process smoother.

1. Analyze your legal responsibilities and business assets

First, you must carefully evaluate your business and assets to determine what you want to insure. Business owners should consult with professionals in the state where they operate to choose what to insure.

For example, an automobile company might want to insure employees for injury, whereas owners of a large distribution company would insure inventory and employees, as required by law.

2. Analyze your risk

Evaluating your risks and liabilities will help you determine which insurance will offer your company the correct type of protection. Careful analysis of business operations, including human resources and facilities, helps determine where the risks are and what should be insured. For example, if your business is on the bottom floor of an office building in a region prone to floods, you will likely opt for comprehensive flood insurance.

3. Consult an insurance broker

An insurance broker is someone who can sell insurance from multiple companies. Insurance brokers work with consumers to compare insurance rates for diverse insurance coverages. Essentially, they act as a middleman between businesses and insurance companies by gathering quotes on behalf of a business. Once they have various options to present, they can then help a business make better and more informed purchasing decisions based on the needs of its customers.

4. Pick an insurance provider

Insurance providers are not all the same. Policies, premiums, and coverage vary, so research the best one to protect your business. Choose a few top providers and compare them by policy coverage, cost, reliability, customer service, and how they handle claims.

5. Cost per employee

When considering the insurance cost, pay special attention to the price per employee. Calculate each employee's income and the cost of their wages. The cost of your business insurance is the average income you receive from each employee to avoid bankruptcy.

Claims Management

A business insurance claim is a formal notification sent by a company to an insurance company to alert them to loss or damage suffered and to request compensation for the loss if the insurance policy covers it. The insurance policy covers certain risks, and a claim should be filed if the loss is related to a risk covered within the policy. On issuing, the insurance provider will investigate the claim. If they approve the claim, the insurance company will issue a payment to the company or a third party affected by the claim on behalf of the company.

Insurance claims management is an insurance carrier's process to ensure claims are paid following regulations. However, it can be challenging because claims regulations often stipulate tight time-lines. The type of claim also plays a role in the regulation process. For example, a medical claim is very different from an E&O insurance claim and, therefore, would have a different regulation process.

Understanding the proper way to file business insurance claims can help you recoup your money on time and get your business operations back to normal as soon as possible.

Steps Involved in Filing a Claim

1. **Consider speaking with a lawyer.** Legal advice might be needed depending on the claim's size. An insurance lawyer can compile claims documentation and offer guidance through the claims process. They can also help resolve any disputes that arise with the insurance adjuster.
2. **Get accounting help.** The services of a forensic accountant can help you properly file the documentation for your business insurance claim. A forensic accountant can help accurately evaluate the losses and what the insurance company should cover in complex cases.
3. **Contact your insurance broker.** Contact your insurance agent or broker to inform them of the situation. They will be able to explain the claim process to you and will ask questions about the incident you're reporting. They will help you fill out the claim form and submit it to the insurance company.

4. **Get evidence.** This process is specific to robbery or natural disasters. Some insurance companies may demand graphic evidence of the disaster reported or a police report in cases of theft or robbery.

5. **Discuss with your insurance adjuster.** Once you file your claim, you should be assigned an adjuster within a few days. The adjuster will investigate your claim and determine how much liability rests with the insurer in your case. The adjuster will require a proof of loss form from you and access to any supporting evidence, such as photos or videos.

6. **Get assessments from a professional.** Obtain quotes and estimates from professionals for repairs. If a storm or fire damages a building owned by your company, call a contractor to come and assess the damage and estimate the repair costs. Try to get at least two estimates.

Employees are the backbone of any organization, and certain violations of employee rights can wreak havoc on an organization. In the next chapter, we will discover how employment practices can pose legal risks and how to manage such risks.

EMPLOYMENT PRACTICES

What will you do as a manager or a business owner when faced with an employee challenge? Is your business in compliance with the latest Employment Standards Acts? How fairly do you treat employees? The answer to these questions lies in the employment practices your company has adopted over time.

Employment practices include all actions relating to your business environment. These practices provide various roles and policies to help businesses function effectively and equip employees with a positive experience. However, the purpose of employment practices may vary depending on what the company wants the practice to target. A good example provides employees with clear expectations, which will help improve morale and give directions.

Moreover, implementing an effective practice will set some ground rules that place everyone in the company on the same page about the business expectations of all employees. The policies resulting from these established practices can help the company avoid litigation and protect the business. For instance, when your company is in a lawsuit for wrongful termination of employment, enough evidence is needed to prove that the employee is aware of the work expectations and has failed to meet them.

From hiring and onboarding to managing your employees' performance, a positive employment practice can make the difference between a healthy business environment and a costly working space. You may have adopted employment practices, but are they the right ones for your business? This chapter will explore the various practices for workplace culture, hiring, and performance management.

HIRING AND ONBOARDING

Having the right employees on your team will determine the success of your business, and choosing the best practices in your selection process can help you achieve that. Employees who contribute at their highest level can enhance productivity, drive growth and innovation, and cultivate a positive work environment.

Nevertheless, adopting a sound recruitment strategy can reduce your chances of missing quality talent and help you make a good hiring decision. It is worth the time and resources to create a standardized hiring procedure to help you select candidates who will best help you achieve your company's goals.

Best Hiring Practices

For the best hiring practices, here are some effective, easily implementable onboarding procedures:

Grow Your Company's Culture

The existence of a supportive culture in your company sends the message that your working environment values its employees and invests in their success. Companies with a strong culture naturally attract highly motivated, skilled workers and can easily retain top talents within their organization.

In a digital world like ours, where job-seekers resort to reviews before choosing, a positive culture will attract good reviews from present employees and customers. So, if your business culture lacks standards, you must address the key drivers.

Streamlined Hiring Process

An efficient onboarding process can save the company resources for recruitment, such as filling vacancies. To ensure your hiring process is efficient, establish a concise and clear job description that accurately reflects the attributes required for the position.

Also, an applicant tracking system (ATS) can be used for repetitive tasks like résumé screening to keep up with time. However, a timeline should be established for each stage so that the hiring process moves coherently.

Promote Employee Referral

Your employees are your greatest assets in finding new skilled hires. They understand your company's culture, values, and objectives, making them the best judges when identifying candidates who can thrive in your company. To promote employee referrals, incentives and rewards like bonuses, extra vacation days, and so on, should be included to motivate employees to recommend highly skilled candidates.

Have Criteria

Clearly outlined minimum requirements for a role are essential in efficiently eliminating undesirable candidates. These requirements may include certifications, educational level, training, work experience, and other skill sets. The above can easily allow companies to screen out undesirable candidates, thus saving time during the hiring process.

Ask the Right Questions

The questions designed for interviews play a role in selecting suitable candidates. Typical questions like "Why do you want the job?" or "What is your greatest strength?" may prove relevant in knowing the candidates' motivation; more insightful interrogations can give an overview of how they fit into the role.

"What is your most challenging project you have completed?" "How do you manage tight deadlines?" are questions that provide specific details about a candidate. Moreover, interviews with peers, supervisors, and hiring managers will provide perspective on the candidate's work style and qualifications for the company.

Anti-Discrimination Policies

Our world has evolved to a place with increased inclusion in the workplace, and implementing anti-discrimination during recruitment is a crucial part of the hiring process. Discrimination in recruitment occurs when a company makes hiring decisions based on a person's gender, age, race, sexual orientation, religion, and other features that do not relate to their ability to perform the job (Vesere, 2024).

Discrimination takes many forms, including prejudice, stereotyping, and unconscious bias. It can also occur at any stage in the selection process, from the job posting to the interview. However, creating a policy that states the company's efforts to prevent discrimination will significantly eliminate the chances of it occurring.

Moreover, these policies should be communicated to all employees and stakeholders, and recruiters should be trained to spot and avoid unconscious bias during selection. To identify them, consistent, clear criteria should be developed for interviews to assess experience, skill, and qualifications. Instead of a subjective assessment, a performance test or work history should be used for job-related criteria.

You also want to ensure that your recruitment process is accessible to disabled candidates. This can be done by installing sign language interpreters, using an easy application process, and having a flexible interview venue and schedule. Also, be on watch to identify any potential discriminatory practices and examine the demographics of the applicants, including the hiring decision, to ensure that the process is unbiased. To this end, conducting regular reviews can keep your business proactive in addressing discrimination concerns, making adjustments, and promoting inclusion in the overall process of selection.

Pre-Employment Screening

In the increased competition in the job market, conducting a thorough prescreening test is crucial for businesses to protect them from bad hires and ensure that the selected employees are the best fit for their roles. Pre-employment screenings are processes for reviewing applicants to select the ones best suited for the role. The information from prescreening checks paints a better and more complete picture of the applicant than what a résumé provides.

Moreover, as an employer, you ensure that new hires are a beneficial addition to your company and are equally of good character. A survey has shown that about 78% of job applicants misrepresent themselves on their résumé, and 56.9% of recruiters need to find out if a candidate has the desired skillset for a position using their résumé (Boatman, 2024). This, in turn, demands a thorough process to filter applicants and develop a satisfied and productive workspace that aligns with your business values.

However, different types of pre-employment screening exist that verify an applicant's experience and skill set, including background checks, skill tests, reference checks, and simulation exercises. Background checks include an investigation into an applicant's criminal records, credit report, sex offender registry, and other information from the database that requires further scrutiny. On the other hand, skill tests will indicate how equipped an applicant is to handle the responsibility of a position and tests their proficiency and ability to handle multiple tasks.

Also, verifying a candidate's previous responsibilities with another company will prove whether an applicant is consistent with the results they claim to have in their résumé and broaden your knowledge about their personality. Stimulation exercises put candidates in a stimulating real-life working space to allow them to experience the job and show their judgment and how they will function in such situations. However, conducting a pre-employment screening requires that you make informed decisions using these steps:

- **Determine the criteria:** Selecting the right candidate begins with defining the specific requirements of the position you are hiring, which also includes pointing out to applicants beforehand the job requirements, company policies, and industrial requirements.

- **Obtain consent:** It is essential to inform applicants how the screening test will go and how the information provided will be used. Under data protection law, employers must inform candidates about their rights and ensure that applicants give their informed consent before the process.
- **Review of application:** This stage involves thoroughly checking the applicant's past work performance, qualifications, total work experience, education, and relevant certifications.
- **Conduct reviews:** Candidates who meet the job requirements should be interviewed to assess their cultural fit, communication skills, and suitability for the position.
- **Other background checks:** Shortlisted candidates from the interviews are checked to verify the accuracy of the information they provide. It includes criminal record checks, education and employment history verification, reference checks, and professional license verification, where applicable.
- **Aptitude assessment:** These tests are performed based on the nature of the role and include cognitive ability tests, technical assessments, and problem-solving exercises.

Employee Contracts

When one accepts a new job offer, one must sign a document outlining the terms of the agreement between them and the company, including information about the salary, job duties, and so on. This employment contract appears as a written document establishing the terms of a working relationship between the employee and the company. Lawyers draft these contracts to show the details of the duties an employee is responsible for and other aspects of employment.

The components of an employment contract include the duration of employment, which often explains how long an employee is supposed to serve in that role. It can be a fixed period or one that changes with promotion to a higher position. Also, a contract may include information about how long an employee is expected to work in a day or a week, the days to be present, and the daily duties they are bound to.

An employment contract should clearly state the employee's hourly, monthly, or yearly compensation. It should also include information about payment schedules, chances of a pay raise, benefits like health insurance, and the company's employee retirement plans. Nevertheless, a well-drafted employment contract should include the company's standard way of resolving conflicts and conclusion details like resignation protocols and termination protection.

WORK CULTURE

Aside from being a common term, many still wonder what work culture entails. A workplace ideally combines a company's ideology and principles, including its total values, traditions, interactions, attitudes, and behaviors. A healthy work culture aligns the company's policies and employees' behaviors with the company's goals and focuses on the well-being of individuals, ensuring that everyone in an organization is satisfied and happy is vital.

Setting up an efficient work culture entails creating a safe and respectful work environment through anti-harassment policies, organizing training programs on workplace conduct, and providing whistleblower protection for employees who report misconduct.

Anti-Harassment Policies

Harassment in the workplace occurs more often than you realize, and it can lead to the loss of skilled talents and the tarnishing of the company's reputation. To avoid this, a company needs to create an effective harassment policy. But what does this policy stand for?

First, it is a policy that aims to prevent and address concerns that violate the dignity of employees. It covers situations involving single or repeated cases of humiliation, intimidation, bullying, or other undesirable conduct toward a person or group of persons. Also, the anti-harassment policy covers misconduct relating to sexual orientation, race, gender, religion, disability, ethnicity, and more.

However, in crafting and sustaining a policy about harassment, the term must encompass a wide range of factors. Thus, when creating, revisiting, or reviewing a harassment policy, prohibited conduct like direct insults, victimization, offensive discussion, or spiteful gossip should be explained thoroughly. Investigate and document all harassment claims and ensure that they are discreetly handled.

Cultural Training Programs

In a modern business environment, individuals tend to focus on what makes them different from one another. Thus, when cross-cultural interaction issues ensue, conflicting perspectives of the arguing parties are highlighted using the interactive aids acquired during training programs.

Intercultural or cultural training in the workplace increases in-house awareness of a company's unique culture. This training equips employees to appreciate, acknowledge, and interact with a different culture in the workplace. Integrating cultural training in a workplace can instigate positive group interaction among employees and eradicate prejudice and discrimination.

Moreover, to design a successful culture training program, you must create a unique framework that makes the program distinct and present it to your employees. It should be delivered repeatedly for an extended period to inculcate the learning in their daily work routines.

PERFORMANCE MANAGEMENT

Businesses are beginning to understand that their management systems must be up-to-date with 21st-century demands to have a competitive advantage in the current market. In light of this trend, several companies are increasingly turning to performance management. By its definition, performance management supports systems built within a company aimed at measuring and improving their employees' performance at work.

This strategic approach to enhanced performance is gaining ground in small and large businesses because it allows individuals, managers, and team members to create an enabling environment to help employees and businesses thrive. They manage these performances by conducting fair and regular evaluations, implementing documented and consistent procedures, and ensuring lawful and respectful termination of employment.

Performance Reviews

A performance review, a formal, regulated assessment system used by companies to evaluate an employee's work performance, can be implemented to ensure that fair evaluations are conducted regularly. The aim is to learn more about the employee's strengths and weaknesses, assist the business in goal setting, and offer constructive feedback for skill development.

Performance reviews can be weekly, monthly, or quarterly, but whatever your choice, a well-planned appraisal will boost your employees' engagement and set the stage for continuous developmental feedback.

Disciplinary Actions

When an employee's behavior becomes unacceptable and has not responded positively to suggestions and advice for improvement, disciplinary actions can occur. A procedure for disciplinary purposes is a formal way in which organizations deal with undesirable behaviors of employees. This process will help you constructively resolve issues, put penalties in place, and ensure your business is covered if sued for unfair dismissal and termination.

Termination Policies

Employee termination can be challenging for everyone involved, but having an internal document outlining this process, including guidelines for addressing performance issues and identifying a reasonable cause for termination, will ensure smooth separation between the employee and the employer.

As Allyns Melendez would say, a termination policy will establish a standard internal guideline for relieving employees to ensure consistency across the company (Rumage, 2024). Whether it is involuntary, voluntary, or mutual termination, having a policy overseeing this will help protect the company's reputation, ensure fairness, and comply with employment laws.

Implementing the best employment practices will help you establish ground rules for your employees and, in turn, boost your business's productivity. However, your company's integrity still depends on product quality, adherence to industrial standards, and management of customer complaints. The next chapter will extensively discuss the factors outlined.

PRODUCT AND SERVICE INTEGRITY

With the business world constantly in a state of change, maintaining the integrity of products and services is crucial for enhancing operational efficiency and shielding oneself from the potential pitfalls of lawsuits and class actions. A company that prioritizes product development or customer service is likely not just aiming to increase revenue; it may proactively mitigate risks that could lead to costly legal disputes. Therefore, one effective strategy to protect your business from legal complications involves strict adherence to industry standards coupled with comprehensive customer service practices. Doing so will preserve your business's reputation and build its long-term success in an environment that is increasingly prone to litigation. What proactive measures can business owners take to prevent lawsuits and class actions by preserving product and service integrity?

PRODUCT DEVELOPMENT

One way you can protect your business from costly lawsuits is by focusing more on product development, and I will divide it into three main aspects so you can get a clearer picture. So, first, let's talk about quality control.

Quality Control

Quality control involves a business's processes to determine their products' quality, safety, and efficacy.

- **Quality:** To determine whether the product is standard or substandard
- **Safety:** To determine whether the product causes harm or danger to the end user
- **Efficacy:** To determine how effective the product is

When quality control is carried out on a product that doesn't meet these basic requirements, the product's production is stopped, and measures can be taken to improve the product.

Why Should Businesses Be Conscious of Quality Control?

Manufacturing a product or delivering a particular service takes a lot of time. It can also be harmful for several reasons. So, here are some reasons why quality control is essential for any business.

- **Compliance:** The government has put out several laws on the manufacturing of products, so once your business is conscious of carrying out quality control on the products being made, you're automatically complying with the rules and regulations that are laid down. However, if you fail to comply with these basic requirements, you could expose your business to the risk of lawsuits and class actions if a defect or flaw is detected in your product.

- **It reduces cost:** Another reason your business should be keen on quality control is because it reduces costs. How does this work? Imagine your products are later detected as low quality; you'd throw them out and lose money. Also, if your customers or employees get affected by your harmful products, it can cost your business a lot of money.

- **Good customer relationship:** One excellent reason your business should invest more in quality control is because it improves customer satisfaction, and whether or not a business will thrive depends on its customers. Once your products meet the standard requirements, you also indirectly satisfy your customers.

- **Improves your brand's Image:** The quality of your products can influence how the public sees your brand. If you want people to purchase from you, you have to make them trust your brand. And how can you do that? Once you deliver top-notch services and products to your customers, they will have no choice but to establish trust in you.

Types of Product Defects

Quality control aims to look for errors or flaws in the product. The types of defects are:

- **Function defect:** This kind of defect reduces or hinders the ability of the product to serve its normal function. A medication intended to alleviate headaches may sometimes fall short in effectiveness, ultimately failing to deliver the necessary relief. This ineffectiveness could indicate potential flaws in the drug's manufacturing process.

- **Visible defect:** This flaw can be seen with the naked eye. For instance, a piece of ripped fabric can be caused by human or machine error. This is an example of an aesthetic flaw.
- **Safety defect:** This kind of flaw is critical because it can cause serious adverse effects like injury or even death to the end user.

Frequent Quality Control Problems: How to Avoid Them

Even when you carry out quality control, you might encounter challenges. Let's look at some general quality control problems you can face in your business and how to avoid them.

- **Inadequate communication:** Businesses facing quality-control problems likely need an adequate communication structure. The error rate can reduce product quality without effective communication or collaboration between the departments. As a business owner, you should make sure each department works together to minimize any problem that could result in lawsuits.
- **Too much dependence on human labor:** When your business relies too much on human labor for procedures that a machine should typically carry out, it can increase the possibility of errors. Even though some manual tasks are unavoidable, every business still needs to utilize automatic solutions and techniques to reduce human workload and improve overall effectiveness.
- **Refusal to implement standards and regulations implement standards and regulations:** Once a business refuses to implement the necessary standards and

protocols, there's every tendency for errors to occur during the manufacturing or fulfillment process. Therefore, as a business owner, you should set up guidelines that must be duly adhered to for every step of the production process.

- **Inadequate documentation:** Your business may have several standards and regulations put in place. Still, finding errors and proposing solutions can be a hassle if proper documentation isn't carried out.

- **Lack of technical know-how:** Imagine a business where the employees lack the proper knowledge of adequate measures to be put in place during production. Or the workers lack the required training to handle the machines. This can lead to impairment in the quality of output. So, the responsibility of every business owner should be to provide their workers with training on how to carry out the production process correctly.

Regulatory Compliance

Regulatory compliance goes a long way in helping business owners avoid lawsuits. Once a business adheres to these rules, it reviews its mode of operation, employment practices, and other aspects. Then, after scrutiny, they can identify and propose solutions to prevent any possible risks. The saying that "it's better to be safe than sorry" can help businesses avoid lawsuits or class actions.

How Can Your Business Benefit From Constant Regulatory Compliance and Legal Audits?

If your business stays abreast of the required industry standards and implements them accordingly, then, as a business owner, you can reduce the possibilities of legal risks and disputes and have a business that operates smoothly.

How Can You Carry Out Regulatory Compliance?

Regulatory compliance is more than a single step—many things must be implemented before it can be perfected. What are the steps involved?

1. **Stay updated on the laws and regulations.** How will you carry them out if you don't know the regulatory compliance rules? Do first things first: You must ensure your business stays up-to-date with the recent laws that apply to your business, location, and mode of operation.

2. **Review internal policies and processes.** The next step is to review your business's policies and processes to ensure they comply with the rules and regulations. Then, discover any areas that may need modification.

3. **Carry out internal audits.** Ensure you conduct a thorough audit of several aspects of your business to determine whether it complies with the standard rules and regulations. You should review contracts, data, or records to ensure efficiency.

4. **Carry a legal expert along.** You must have a legal expert helping your business. They can provide insights and help your company navigate the legal world.

5. **Identify areas that do not comply with the standard rules.** Next, identify areas where your business needs to catch up with the updated regulations and make adjustments where necessary.

6. **Implement an action plan.** You can then map out a strategic plan to deal with areas that do not adhere to the rules. Assign tasks, give them specific deadlines, and tackle the most important ones first so that you can correct the problems quickly.

Product Labeling

As simple as a label can be, if the standard labeling requirements are not adhered to, it can result in intense legal risks. Therefore, any product that can cause danger or harm to consumers must come with a warning label. The labels must be specific about the risk inherent in the product and how users can avoid any problem. You can include graphics in the labels or warnings in different languages. Also, you should carefully review the labels to ensure you provide accurate and precise information to the consumers. For instance, a food business that produces a product with nuts inside and refuses to include it in the label may face a lawsuit if a consumer has an allergic reaction.

CUSTOMER SERVICE

Every business owner looks for one way or another to avoid lawsuits, and prioritizing customers is a very effective way of achieving that. Once a business can satisfy its customers, it has taken a big step toward reducing the possibility of legal disputes. Even if an issue arises with one of your customers and they log a complaint, how you handle the matter determines whether or not the problem will escalate. Providing good customer service doesn't just protect the image of your business; it also reduces the chances of any legal threat. Ensuring good customer service isn't limited to putting a smile on your customer's face; it's a tactic for avoiding legal risks.

Handling Complaints

Let's look at a quick example to show how you can promptly handle every customer's complaint. Let's imagine that you run an online business selling perfumes and deodorants.

One of your customers ordered a box of perfume, but regrettably, the glass bottle likely shattered during transit, leading to the customer's frustration upon receiving the package. Consequently, this dissatisfied customer opted to lodge a formal complaint. How should you handle this situation? You can follow the steps outlined below.

- **Be attentive.** The customer files a complaint that they're angry because they ordered a costly perfume. It probably came in cheap packaging, making it shatter during delivery. Instead of arguing with them, why don't you use that feedback to upgrade your product's packaging?
- **Show empathy.** Take responsibility for your mistake and tell the customer you understand their point of view.
- **Apologize.** Tell the customer that you are sorry for falling short of their expectations and thank them for being kind enough to call your attention to the matter.
- **Ask questions.** After apologizing, ask the customer what you can do to make them feel better.
- **Talk to your team.** You can explain the problem to your team.
- **Make a plan to address the matter.** In this step, you can either re-send another perfume to the customer or give them a refund.
- **Keep up with the customer.** Once the issue has been resolved, you can contact the customer to learn about their experience while shopping with you.
- **Document the incidence.** Write down the interaction you had with the customer. After a while, if you discover that customers constantly complain about broken perfume bottles due to improper packaging, you can take active measures to resolve the problem quickly.

Warranties and Returns

Another way you can ensure product and service integrity is by enforcing warranty and return policies in your business. So how can you do this?

Let the Customers Know What They're Signing Up for

- Every product must have a precise outline of what the warranty does and does not cover.
- The customer must be aware of the warranty period, which helps to prevent any misunderstandings.
- Customers should be pleased when making warranty claims to ensure prompt resolution.

Have a Clear Return Policy

- Be kind enough with your return period so customers can have ample time to review what they buy.
- Make sure that the return procedure is stress-free to prevent any forms of customer frustration or possible quarrels.
- Customers should be aware of the conditions in which the products must be returned to prevent any form of misunderstanding.

Legal Compliance

- Ensure that your warranty and return policies follow the regulatory bodies' rules.
- Ensure you stay up-to-date with the policies on warranty and returns in case there are any modifications to the rules.

Customer Feedback

The laws guiding consumer protection are stringent; once a business fails to comply with them, it can face intense penalties. However, once a business prioritizes customer feedback, it can reduce the possibilities of legal risks and protect its operation.

Feedback from a customer can be valuable insight that boosts a company's mode of operations. Once you can review these complaints, you can make strategic decisions that can improve the overall functioning of your business.

Once your business offers a strong product and reliable services, you've taken the right steps to protect it from expensive lawsuits. For instance, in a furniture store, if a customer is unhappy with a product and complains, getting positive feedback in return shows the business has made the right choice to keep that customer and their money. Good products and services lower the risk of legal problems and improve the business's reputation, helping it succeed. If you improve your products as well as improve customer service, you'll avoid legal issues and build a brand that people will trust and like. The next chapter will focus on creating and managing contracts as a business owner.

CONTRACT MANAGEMENT

C ontracts are crucial to modern businesses. Whether you are a startup or an established business expanding its base by entering into a partnership with another company, contracts are legal agreements that outline everyone's responsibility in the deal. Contract management has proved perfect, especially when efficiency is critical to a successful business. It has become a hot topic recently, but have you ever wondered how contract management shakes up the way companies do business? Why is this so important?

Contract management is the overall process of efficiently planning and managing contracts with entities like vendors, partners, employees, and customers at all stages of their engagement with your company. It comprises the procedures for managing a legally binding agreement from initiation to execution (Bryce, 2023). Your company's visibility, compliance, and control level can be significantly influenced by how your business manages its contracts, starting with the system it uses and how both teams work.

Setting up a standardized and collaborative contract management system is crucial because it gets all stakeholders working on the same ground and leaves no room for the phrase "no surprises." Handling contracts end-to-end influences the outcomes of agreements by designing a process that helps you extract maximum value from a contract. Also, everyone on the team knows what is expected of them when a contract is managed well, and there is foresight of what the business should expect down the road.

DRAFTING CONTRACTS

A contract must pass through these seven stages before you sign it off to ensure that your business achieves a favorable negotiated outcome and maximizes opportunities to strengthen its position:

1. **Initiation:** When a new partnership, product, or service is launched, it is vital to have a transparent process that everyone will follow. This process starts with capturing the requirements, details of potential stakeholders, and sign-off agreements. Surprisingly, these controllable details are often not covered accurately, making the rest of the process difficult if not considered.
2. **Contract negotiation:** At this stage, good contract management ensures that both sides reach a rewarding and beneficial mutual agreement that is attainable. Most contract managers focus on cost reduction and control, but neither party should feel it is losing. Actions needed at this stage include preferred supplier selection, legal review, and contract draft issuing.
3. **Execution:** Once an agreement is reached, finalized documents must be signed by the parties involved. The document should include all agreed-upon changes and be shared with the key stakeholders.

4. **Startup:** This is a fundamental stage that requires documenting key features of the contract and adding them to the central register. Although it can be overlooked when trying to get the contract up and running, considering this stage will help you assign responsibilities to ongoing contract management.

5. **Monitoring:** Contract monitoring involves regular check-ins and ongoing performance assessments to ensure milestones and targets are met, especially in expense and revenue. Monitoring also helps businesses ensure total compliance, especially in a world where regulations change quickly. Contract management actions at this stage include automated obligation tracking, performance measurement using checklists, and commercial review conduct.

6. **Renewal:** Renewal offers an excellent opportunity for better negotiation terms, cost reduction, and extended relationships with other parties. It is the stage when discussions about the value received and continuation of terms are triggered, but businesses often fail to make the most out of it. Having a clear line in sight for all contract renewals is crucial for maximizing the necessary value from your agreements and minimizing risk. Also, remember to access competing parties for price and level of delivery and internal users for feedback on performance.

7. **Completion:** Although this stage is usually ignored, it may be necessary—you never know what information and records might be relevant. Actions required in this stage include recording contract performance, thoroughly checking for gaps in information recording, and moving contract records to the archive.

Clear Terms

To have a binding contract, a business's written agreements must be clear and specific in wording, including putting every ambiguous clause and any particular action in plain language. So, to make contract terms as straightforward as possible, thoroughly and carefully review them to identify inconsistencies or errors. Pay close attention to definitions, deliverables, scope, payment deadlines, warranties, and liabilities, as they are often the most critical aspects of a contract.

When writing contract terms, use precise language, avoiding jargon, professional terms, and acronyms that all parties may not understand. If you must use them, define them consistently throughout the contract to prevent generating different interpretations and implications. For instance, instead of "soon," a specific time and date should be used.

Moreover, another way to ensure that contract terms are clear is to ask questions and seek feedback from other parties involved. Refrain from assuming everyone understands the term the same way you do. Invite them to seek clarification on any uncertain point and ask them questions about concerns arising in the negotiation. By doing this, misunderstandings or miscommunications likely to result in disputes in the long run are avoided.

Also, it is advisable to use relatable scenarios to explain and illustrate how the contract is applicable in practice. The scenarios can clarify the terms' meaning and intentions and the parties' expectations. This clarification approach can identify and address potential issues, concerns, and risks. A typical example is using industrial-based scenarios to illustrate how a payment term will work, how the deliverables will be measured and evaluated, and how warranties will be enforced.

Legal Review

As a business owner, you can avoid exposing your business to potential risk by integrating legal review into your contract management process. Contract reviews can help you identify and analyze the critical factors for negotiation within an agreement, thus allowing all parties involved to recheck and make mutually favorable adjustments. It ensures a contract is legal, feasible, and meets its original need.

Producing a legally enforceable agreement involves reading and comprehending a contract written by an expert attorney or a legal professional in contract reviews. Most importantly, most contracts can be used for internal and corporate transactions of the company, but regardless of whichever purpose they are used for, ensure that they can stand up in court against any charges through legal reviews.

Contract review occurs in stages, beginning with a thorough preview of the contract by in-house counsel to find the purpose of the contract and the expectations from both parties. It should be established that the draft has the following factors:

- Commercial protection.
- The duration of the contract includes the notice period, initiation period, and termination provisions.
- Determinants for payment include when a payment starts or what a party will do to get paid.
- Payment terms involve ensuring the payment style fits the company's policy and both parties agree.

The next thing the legal teams look out for is potential risks with the contract type that can jeopardize the whole agreement in the long run. During this review, warranties can be added to protect the parties involved. Likewise, data protection is accessed, and an inquiry is made to know whether the contract made provisions for intellectual property.

After the legal team has identified the risk that a contract will deal with, warranties, indemnity, and limitations of liability should be looked into. The warranties the contract will consider should be precise and focused on authorizations, titles, and licenses relevant to the contract. On the other hand, indemnity should be included only in contracts dealing with intellectual property, destruction of data, or regulation compliance. However, limitation of liability is used only for liabilities where warranties and indemnity are breached.

Dispute Resolution Clauses

A written contract has the advantage of providing more clarity about the parties and can help prevent misunderstandings. Even if a dispute arises, there is already a process to address it. Also, any contractual relationship must have a standardized and agreed-upon process for resolving disputes.

The dispute resolution clause in a contract expresses how both parties intend to work together. This approach generally lowers cost and time and helps preserve relationships after a dispute. However, no one dispute resolution clause applies to all types of contracts, but whichever one is chosen must have content that is carefully considered and drafted to meet all possible dispute needs of the parties involved.

Dispute resolution clauses should clearly state each party's rights and obligations during a dispute. They outline the process both parties must follow, which is streamlined to reflect their concerns and legally enables resolution. Also, a good mediation clause should allow for the ongoing performance of the contract duties while resolving a dispute and address what happens if the dispute resolution process becomes unsuccessful.

Most importantly, it should be decided when making a contract whether a dispute resolution clause will survive the termination of the contract. Clarity should be provided on the avenue for enforcement of the agreement reached through the dispute resolution process—usually tribunals or courts. Nevertheless, the dispute resolution clause should be specific in what is considered a dispute, the scope of the dispute about the contract, and situations where the clause will be initiated.

MANAGING CONTRACTS

When two or more companies wish to do business with each other and go ahead to sign terms of an agreement that both parties will fulfill, legal accountability is held between both teams, and a contract manager is required to read and sign the agreement. As indicated above, this task requires lots of scrutiny that goes through stages, making it the domain of lawyers rather than entrepreneurs. When legal experts manage contracts, it ensures the agreement is airtight and relieves entrepreneurs of that duty to focus on other things. The following procedures are considered during contract management:

Contract Database

Maintaining an organized system for managing contracts should be prioritized to keep track of the process and performance of contracts. Most contract managers use contract management systems, comprehensive platforms in which businesses streamline their contract processes. Contracts should be appropriately categorized to avoid substantial risk to your business resulting from compliance issues, missed deadlines, or unnoticed auto-renewals. However, the guidelines below will aid in organizing your contracts effectively, helping you make the most of your contractual relationship:

1. **Identify your core goals.** Before organizing your contract management system, you need to identify your primary goals. Motives can vary widely, but some examples are enhancing productivity, improving contract performance, achieving a transparent relationship, and reducing risk.

2. **Plan a system.** Once your goals are in place, it is time to decide the key functionalities you want your system to do for you. These include drafting contracts, managing negotiations, enforcing compliance, and tracking deadlines. Ensure that you create precise data categorization when designing the system.

3. **Implement the system.** Drafting a theory isn't enough! The next step should be implementation, which is where some software can help you. This software can function like enacting your contract management system or giving you access to a digital contract analytics tool.

4. **Maintain your system over time.** Contract management systems require regular upkeep and revision. Revisiting them ensures that your contract processes evolve with your industry's needs. Various ways to maintain them include updating contractual terms, revising outdated clauses, and scaling the storage system.

Performance Monitoring

Never get carried away by the initial excitement of signing a new contract. The real deal is to ensure that the agreed-upon terms are carried out, which will require continual, well-structured monitoring and assessment. Measuring a contract's success requires vigilance and evaluation, even after the signing phase. Thus, contract performance monitoring assesses how the parties involved in an agreement have met their contractual obligations.

Systematic and regular evaluation of contractual terms remains critical for successful business relationships because it ensures that future contracts are successful. However, in accessing contract performance, four things have to be considered and thoroughly evaluated:

Establishment of Contract Performance Metrics

In setting up a successful contract performance evaluation, the basics must be firmly laid out in the pre-signing stage, which starts with establishing clear contract performance metrics. The metrics should be mutually favorable, agreed upon, and written down as a primary yardstick for measuring the delivery of the contract. Regularity of services, ongoing costs, measurement of timelines, and incident response time ensure that a legally bound agreement is delivered as expected.

Collection and Analysis of Data

Once the metrics are established, they must be continuously and closely monitored to ensure accuracy in performance measurement. This step requires collecting data at regular intervals to assess each party's progress in meeting the terms of the agreement.

Communication of the Result

One of the best practices in contract management is generating a regular contract performance report at a predetermined time. It communicates the process to both parties and allows for corrections and improvements. Moreover, creating contract lifecycle management tools has made generating results seamless.

Spotting and Implementing Improvement

Contract performance review is the last step in the assessment process and is crucial because it affects future contracts. A well-performed periodic review of contract performance results can help businesses more accurately identify trends, weaknesses, and opportunities for improvement, allowing them to stay at the competitive edge.

Renewals and Termination

The original agreement should be reviewed before initiating a contract renewal or termination. Look at the clauses that specifically addressed the duration, renewal options, notice period, penalties, and termination rights. Ensure you understand your rights and acknowledge the potential risk in renewing or terminating the contracts. After concluding with the choice of either terminating or restoring, the next thing is to communicate your intentions to the other party, and depending on the kind of contract, it can be in the form of a formal letter or a simple email.

If your supplier agrees to your renewal or termination, there may be a need to negotiate the process. For instance, when renewing a contract, you may need to discuss new terms, deliverables, timelines, and fees. Likewise, you should reach an agreement on final deliverables, obligations, and payments in contract termination. After reaching a deal, you can implement the renewal or termination, which may require you to approve a new contract, an amendment, or a termination. Document a copy of all the contract renewal or termination processes and securely store them for future use.

Efficient contract management is a necessary process that begins with contract creation, execution, and maintenance. Contracts are vital for protecting a business against risk and ensuring that all parties are satisfied. However, as mentioned earlier, indemnity is a crucial security for contracts that contribute intellectual property to an agreement, and it is considered depending on the choice of contract type. The next chapter will discuss IP portfolio management and licensing extensively.

GROOVESHARK: A SOBERING STORY

"Knowledge itself is power."

— FRANCIS BACON

There's no shortage of examples of businesses that had to close their doors because of legal issues, and we've seen several examples already, but perhaps the case of Grooveshark is one of the best examples of why *The Enterprise Shield* is so necessary.

Grooveshark was a music streaming platform, and it was very popular for a while. It was founded by a pair of college students who were learning as they went along, and the problem there is that learning the legalities as you go is a very risky business. They faced financial issues and had a lack of investment, which also contributed to their downfall, but one major problem was that they crossed the line when it came to copyright. They ended up being sued by several record labels, and as a result, their app was banned (Failory, n.d.). Had they known how to navigate the legalities of setting up and running a business better, this may never have happened, and it's likely that the company would have been very successful today.

I wrote this book because it's vital for business owners to know and understand the legal landscape, and doing so could make the difference between success and failure for your business. With your knowledge growing with every turn of the page, I'd like to ask you to take a moment to help other business owners connect with this information—and that's as easy as leaving a short review.

By leaving a review of this book on Amazon, you'll make it easier to find, and more business owners will be able to enrich their understanding of the potential legal issues they may encounter before it's too late.

Business owners (as you know, being one yourself) want to know this information; it's just not that easy to find everything in one place. Together, we can change that!

Thank you so much for your support. No business deserves to fail simply because of a lack of knowledge, and we can make sure fewer do.

Scan the QR code below

INTELLECTUAL PROPERTY PROTECTION

Intellectual property (IP) protection is a legal formality and a crucial shield against potential losses. It encompasses the legal rights of individuals and companies over their creations, such as inventions, designs, brands, and processes. Without these protections, original ideas can be copied or used without permission, leading to potential financial and reputational damage. This underscores the vital need for businesses and individuals to manage and protect what they create.

Take Sam, an inventor who spent years creating a new app to help people manage their personal finances. After a lot of hard work, Sam launched the app, which was well-received. But just as things were going well, another company released a similar app to Sam's.

Sam, realizing the vulnerability of his invention without IP protection, sought the advice of an IP lawyer. The lawyer explained the importance of patents and trademarks, which was a turning point for Sam. He followed the advice and secured a patent for his app and a trademark for his brand, a move that gave him confidence as well as a competitive edge.

With the protection of his IP, Sam could confidently add unique features to his app, making it stand out in the market. His IP protection secured his position in the market and increased his earnings. Sam's success story is a good lesson on the pivotal role of intellectual property in business security and growth.

Sam's story underscores the empowerment that comes with understanding and prioritizing IP protection. By doing so, entrepreneurs and businesses can protect their innovations, maintain a competitive advantage, and ensure their creative work leads to lasting success.

This chapter will outline all the essential aspects of IP that a business owner must understand.

IP PORTFOLIO MANAGEMENT

IP portfolio management is a strategic approach to managing a collection of IP assets. The first step is identifying and cataloging these assets, which is essential for a comprehensive understanding of your IP landscape. A good starting point is to create a detailed inventory of all your intellectual property. This may encompass trademarks, patents, copyrights, and trade secrets. Once you have thoroughly documented these assets, you can assess their value and determine the most effective strategies for protection.

Identifying IP Assets: Cataloging All Intellectual Property Assets

Cataloging your intellectual property (IP) assets is essential for clearly visualizing your portfolio and gaining insights into its strengths and weaknesses. Creating a detailed spreadsheet is an effective method for organizing this information. In your spreadsheet, include vital details such as:

- **Type of IP:** E.g., patents, trademarks, copyrights
- **Registration status:** Registered, pending, or unregistered
- **Renewal deadlines**
- **Associated rights or limitations**

This spreadsheet serves not only as a record but also as a valuable analytical tool to assess the strength of your portfolio.

Utilizing Specialized Software

In addition to spreadsheets, consider using specialized software designed for IP management. These tools can streamline the cataloging process, automate reminders for renewal deadlines, and facilitate tracking essential milestones. Many platforms also integrate analytics features, helping you evaluate the market position of your IP assets. Such insights make it easier to strategize future investments or modify your IP approach effectively.

In summary, a well-structured cataloging process utilizing spreadsheets and specialized software is crucial for managing and optimizing intellectual property assets.

Filing and Registration: Ensuring Proper Filing and Registration of IP

Proper IP filing and registration are essential to securing your rights over various assets. Each type of asset has its own specific filing process, which requires meticulous attention to detail to ensure compliance and protection.

Patents

Filing for a patent necessitates a thorough and detailed description of the invention and a demonstration of its novelty and utility to meet the criteria for approval. This process typically involves preparing complex documentation, including claims and drawings, which can be challenging to understand. Therefore, it is advisable to seek the assistance of a qualified patent attorney who can provide expertise and guidance throughout the patent office's requirements, increasing the likelihood of successful registration.

Trademarks

Unlike patents, trademarks require distinctiveness and must be directly associated with specific goods or services. Conducting a comprehensive trademark search ensures your desired mark is consistent with existing registrations. Engaging legal guidance during this process can help you anticipate any potential objections, enhancing the chances of a successful application.

Maintenance of IP Rights

Once your IP is registered, diligently tracking renewal dates becomes critical to maintaining your rights. You must renew to avoid losing legal protections associated with your IP. Establishing reminders for renewal deadlines or utilizing IP management software can simplify compliance and ensure your rights remain intact.

In summary, taking the proper steps for filing and registration, including seeking legal assistance and staying organized with renewals, is crucial for effectively protecting your intellectual property.

Monitoring and Enforcement: Regularly Monitoring for IP Infringements and Taking Enforcement Actions

Monitoring your IP is as crucial as the initial registration process. Regular vigilance is necessary to identify potential infringements, such as unauthorized use of trademarks or unauthorized copying of copyrighted materials. To streamline this process, you can leverage technology by setting up alerts for unauthorized use of your IP or by employing a specialized monitoring service that tracks IP violations.

Responding to Infringements

When an infringement is discovered, you need to respond swiftly and decisively. The initial step often involves sending cease-and-desist letters to the offending parties, clearly outlining the nature of the infringement and demanding that they stop their infringing activities. This communication can sometimes lead to negotiations that resolve the issue amicably. However, pursuing legal action may be necessary if negotiations fail or if the infringement is severe. This could involve filing a lawsuit to assert your rights and seek remedies for the breach.

Proactive Enforcement

Proactively monitoring and enforcing your IP rights is crucial. It protects your IP and serves as a deterrent against future infringements. A visible commitment to enforcing your IP rights enhances your reputation as a diligent rights holder, reinforcing the value of your IP in the marketplace.

In summary, robust IP portfolio management should integrate monitoring and enforcement strategies into a comprehensive approach that supports innovation, safeguards competitive advantages, and maximizes returns on your intellectual assets.

IP LICENSING

Licensing is an effective strategy for managing IP, enabling you to monetize your assets by granting others the right to use them under specific conditions. A well-crafted licensing agreement is essential to outline the terms clearly, ensuring that both parties understand their rights and obligations. This approach generates revenue and broadens your IP's reach, encouraging collaboration and innovation.

Licensing Agreements: Drafting Clear and Enforceable Licensing Agreements

When drafting a licensing agreement, clarity and specificity are paramount. The document should comprehensively detail the scope of the license, explicitly outlining how the IP can be used, the duration of the license, and the geographic territories covered. For instance, if you license patented technology to a manufacturer, you must specify whether they can modify the technology or are required to use it in its original form. Additionally, include restrictions on using your IP to prevent unauthorized exploitation or misapplication, stipulating that the IP cannot be sublicensed without your consent.

Engaging legal professionals specializing in IP law when drafting licensing agreements is highly advisable. Their expertise ensures that the contract is enforceable and adequately protects your interests. They can also provide insights on industry standards and potential pitfalls, customizing the agreement to fit the specific nuances of your intellectual assets and the intended market.

Royalty Management: Monitoring and Collecting Royalties

Effective royalty management is essential for maximizing earnings from your IP. Once a licensing agreement is established, closely monitoring royalty payments and ensuring timely collections become vital. A structured approach emphasizing organization, communication, and adaptability can help streamline this process.

Establish a Monitoring System

Create a plan or calendar to track expected royalty dates using a wall calendar or electronic planner.

Set Up Payment Collection Process

Implement a straightforward procedure for timely payment collection. Send friendly reminders to licensees a week before payments are due. Create a checklist for each payment period, including:

- Verifying due dates
- Confirming receipt of sales reports
- Ensuring payments are made

Maintain Effective Communication

Keep lines of communication open with licensees for clarity and transparency. Schedule regular check-ins to discuss:

- Performance metrics
- Royalty calculations and product performance

Build a positive relationship to encourage sharing sales trends and market changes.

Address Disputes Promptly

Handle disputes concerning royalty payments quickly and professionally. Clearly outline responsibilities in the licensing agreement from the outset. Maintain thorough documentation to facilitate resolution if issues arise.

Approach Disputes With a Solution-Oriented Mindset

Focus on finding a way forward rather than casting blame. Meet to discuss specific issues and listen actively to licensees' perspectives.

Clarify Licensing Agreement Terms

Discuss any points regarding royalty calculations that need to be clarified in detail. Provide examples to illustrate calculations and factors affecting final payments to prevent misunderstandings.

Revisit the Licensing Agreement Regularly

Periodically assess and adjust the licensing agreement to reflect market changes and partnership dynamics. Renegotiate rates based on market trends when necessary.

Monitor Market Trends

Observe market behavior to inform pricing and licensing decisions. Consider raising royalty rates if demand for a product increases.

Integrate Technology

Use software solutions to track sales, manage contracts, and audit royalty payments. Leverage technology for real-time sales data to respond to market demand changes efficiently.

Maintain Relationships With Legal Advisors

Work with legal experts to draft solid agreements and navigate disputes. A proactive legal approach safeguards your interests and ensures compliance with licensing terms.

Implementing a structured and organized approach to royalty management, maintaining open communication, and leveraging technology can ensure a smooth and effective process for managing and collecting royalties.

Dispute Resolution: Handling IP-Related Disputes Effectively

Disputes are common in IP management, arising from various reasons, including disagreements over licensing agreements, claims of infringement, or confusion regarding usage rights. Given the prevalence of these conflicts, having a solid plan to manage them is crucial. A well-structured dispute-resolution strategy helps resolve conflicts smoothly, reducing stress and minimizing potential costs.

Drafting Clear Agreements

When creating a licensing agreement, you'll need to include specific terms regarding resolving disputes. Methods such as mediation and arbitration can provide structured solutions to problems without resorting to costly and time-consuming court proceedings. Mediation involves a neutral third party facilitating discussions between the conflicting parties to reach a mutual agreement. In contrast, arbitration entails a neutral individual making a binding decision that both sides agree to follow, which can swiftly conclude the dispute but may relinquish some control over the outcome.

Importance of Preparation

Preparation plays a pivotal role in effective dispute resolution. Take the time to understand the terms of your agreements thoroughly; this knowledge can help identify potential conflict areas before they escalate into more significant issues. For instance, if a licensing agreement contains vague or unclear sections, addressing these inconsistencies upfront can save time and energy later. When both parties have clear expectations, it often leads to quicker resolutions.

Communication as a Prevention Tool

Open lines of communication are vital in preventing disputes from arising or worsening. Regular check-ins with licensees or partners can create an environment where concerns are shared openly before they escalate into more significant problems. Adopting a collaborative mindset during conflicts is also essential; instead of focusing on winning an argument, aim to find solutions that work for all parties involved. This approach can help maintain healthy business relationships and build long-lasting partnerships.

Transparency and Proactivity

Discussing potential conflict areas during the agreement phase can cultivate a culture of transparency. For example, if you anticipate issues regarding how a product will be marketed, openly discussing expectations with your licensing partners can help establish clear boundaries, reducing the likelihood of disputes occurring later on.

Responding to Disputes

When a dispute does arise, being prepared can make a significant difference. Start by carefully reviewing the licensing agreement, focusing on what both parties initially agreed to and identifying applicable terms. This step grounds your understanding and helps outline your subsequent actions. If mediation is included in the agreement, consider suggesting that approach first, as it allows for a more relaxed and open discussion.

Detailed notes can also facilitate effective dispute resolution by documenting essential conversations, agreements, and any modifications made over time. Maintaining precise records provides a reference point should problems arise later. For instance, if a partner asserts they have the right to use a logo in a particular way, you can refer to the agreement. Having well-organized documentation shows you take the situation seriously and are prepared to discuss it factually.

Moving to Arbitration

Consider transitioning to arbitration if mediation does not lead to an effective resolution. Although this step may seem daunting, remember that the goal is to resolve the conflict. Both parties must agree on the chosen arbitrator, ideally someone well-versed in your industry's nuances or the dispute's specific aspects. This expertise increases the likelihood that the decision will be fair and relevant.

Regularly Review Your Plan

Finally, routinely review and update your dispute-resolution plan. As business practices evolve, so should your conflict resolution strategies. For example, if new licensing trends emerge in your industry, adapt your agreements accordingly. Continually refining your dispute resolution approach enables you to stay ahead and avoid future conflicts.

In conclusion, maintaining good relationships while resolving disputes is paramount. A strong, well-worded dispute resolution plan is critical to successful IP management, helping prevent long, costly legal battles and allowing all parties to focus on collaboration rather than conflict. You can effectively handle IP-related disputes and strengthen your business relationships by establishing clear agreements, fostering open communication, and investing in careful preparation.

Managing IP effectively requires diligence, knowledge, and a proactive approach. From cataloging your assets to drafting solid licensing agreements, each step plays an essential role in protecting and enhancing the value of your IP in a competitive environment. By implementing thorough licensing practices, maintaining transparent communication, and being prepared for potential disputes, you can successfully navigate IP management's complexities, ultimately engendering innovation and growth within your business.

REGULATORY COMPLIANCE

A ccording to records, nearly 50% of companies interacting with customers online are requested to provide proof of cybersecurity when submitting Requests for Proposals (RFP) (Veritas, 2024). What does that tell you? Maintaining regulatory compliance is now critical in securing your company because the risks resulting from noncompliance are far too significant to ignore.

Ideally, it can be challenging to keep up with changing regulations in your industry, let alone being compliant. This issue has made regulatory compliance a complex and ever-evolving problem within businesses of all sizes. However, failure to comply with regulatory requirements will lead to fines, prosecution, and reputational damages. Another angle to it is that most businesses see regulatory compliance as a daunting task. Still, fortunately, the guidelines in this chapter will help you keep your business compliant with industrial standards. By understanding what regulatory compliance entails and how it can affect your business, you can better plan strategies that will help your company stay ahead in meeting legal requirements.

UNDERSTANDING REGULATIONS

The critical factor in service delivery is customer interaction and how their data is handled and stored. It all lies in customers' trust when you use their data for authorized purposes and to protect their details. As a result of negligence and increased hacking incidents capable of compromising weak systems, companies now must adhere to strict rules.

Compliance with these regulations comes into play—you must keep up with the latest laws and standards that apply to your industry, whether state, federal, or international. It also involves implementing internal processes that monitor employees' behavior toward data handling and keep track of a customer's data. Staying on top of these unique rules in your industry helps you avoid fines and provides financial security for the company.

Moreover, regulatory compliance is essential for businesses. Knowing its difference from other legal concerns will help you navigate them better, set priorities, and protect your business from legal consequences. Also, customers tend to relate better and have higher expectations for companies that comply with the required standards, making it easier to build loyalty when your business demonstrates compliance.

Industry-Specific Regulations

Global connectivity and digitalization have made data protection an integral concern for businesses, cutting through all sectors. Consequently, ensuring a high level of standard security for business data has become an increasing necessity, but it can be very confusing to determine which regulation applies to your industry. As much as each industry has unique regulatory compliance, the requirements typically remain the same across all boards intending to protect users' data and business information. Here are the industrial-specific compliance requirements applicable to businesses:

Healthcare

Strict compliance with regulations is absolutely necessary in the healthcare industry, owing to the sensitive nature of patient health status information and the potential consequences of a data breach. Healthcare compliance regulations are designed to protect patients' data while facilitating the processing of relevant information. Thus, two key compliances crucial for the healthcare industry include the Health Information Technology for Economic and Clinical Health Act (HITECH Act) and the Health Insurance Portability and Accountability Act (HIPAA).

HIPAA is a compliance rule regulating the disclosure and usage of health information to uphold patient confidentiality and privacy (Team, 2024). It has a privacy rule establishing national standards for handling and protecting patients' medical and other personal information, covering institutions like health plans, healthcare providers, and healthcare clearinghouses. At the same time, HIPAA security rules set standards for securing electronically protected health information and ensuring that healthcare institutions implement administrative, physical, and technical measures to protect patients' data against threats, disclosures, and unauthorized access.

However, the HITECH Act is implemented to promote the adoption of health information and the use of ethics across medical devices. Its breach notification rule demands that healthcare institutions and their business partners notify the secretary of health and human services to avoid data-breach cases. This rule also requires these institutions to conduct risk assessments to determine the potential for compromised information. Meanwhile, the meaningful use regulations encourage the sensible use and application of electronic health records by offering financial advantages to qualified healthcare providers.

Education

Businesses in the edutech sector must adhere to compliance requirements to thrive ethically. Educational institutions handle critical student information, such as research data, and must comply with the Children's Online Privacy Protection Act (COPPA) and the Federal Educational Rights and Privacy Act (FERPA).

FERPA is a federal statute to safeguard the confidentiality of students' educational records. This law provides essential privacy rights for parents and students, regulating disclosure and access to educational documentation. Moreover, COPPA creates a safe and secure online environment for all students worldwide. Strict rules are placed on websites for children under 13 to obtain parental consent for collecting identities, using collected data for decision-making, and disclosing personal information to third-party websites.

Logistics

Compliance with regulations in the logistics industry is vital for safe global transportation practices. These laws promote the protection of sensitive data and uphold the integrity of supply-chain productions. The two major compliance laws governing logistics are the Sarbanes-Oxley Act (SOX) and Service Optimization Controls (SOC).

SOX is responsible for ensuring strict accuracy and transparency in financial statements, indirectly managing how companies manage their supply chains. SOC is a guideline for secured data handling and building trust among crucial B2B holders. It also comprises reports controlling factors like data availability, data-processing integrity, security, and customer confidentiality.

Finances

Since the finance sector is the prime target for hackers, it is governed by more stringent regulations than others. The two compliance measures that all fintech must take to ensure sustainability include Anti-Money Laundering Regulations (AML) and Payment Card Industry Data Security Standards (PCI DSS). The AML secrecy rules demand that financial institutions establish compliance programs that detect and prevent laundering and terrorist financial activities. The compliance rules include reporting suspicious activity, reporting currency exchanges, and performing customer due diligence.

Compliance Requirements

Operating a business that does not adhere to compliance regulations can be costly, risky, and time-consuming. Although not all companies have specialized roles dedicated to compliance officers, the responsibilities can still be delegated to available personnel in appropriate positions in the company. However, to ensure regulatory compliance in your business, you must adhere to general best practices.

First, your company must stay on top of regulatory compliance changes at the industrial and jurisdictional levels. Next, it should create and maintain a code of conduct that inculcates a culture of compliance in the workplace, thus encouraging ethical and fair practices. Also, documentation of the compliance process is necessary and can be done by clearly outlining the roles and responsibilities of staff involved in adequate compliance management.

Nevertheless, training employees in compliance management is essential and can be conducted through training sessions, workshops, and periodic assessments of compliance requirements. This periodic review helps correct the policy's weaknesses and ensures compliance regulations are current with every change in your business environment. Also, all these processes can be automated, depending on the organization's scope.

IMPLEMENTING COMPLIANCE PROGRAMS

With governments and authorities worldwide constantly revising and enforcing laws to eliminate a range of illicit activities from the corporate world, including market manipulation, fraud, and money laundering, implementing compliance programs has never been more critical. Your business's regulatory compliance policy is the blueprint for operating within the jurisdiction applicable to your industry. Fighting the employees after an event of compliance lapse is no longer satisfactory. Instead, the compliance department can consider mitigating potential risks by developing a regulatory compliance strategy or policy.

Policies and Procedures

However, the elements of your strategy would depend mainly on the sector of your business and the size of the organization, but the basic steps in developing a solid compliance program include:

- **Define the goals.** You should be able to identify the function of the compliance program you intend to set up.

For example, reduce the amount of money the company spends on penalties, save time on retrospective investigations accompanying failings, or improve the use of compliant actions among employees.

- **Align with your corporate culture.** Having a compliance program that aligns with the cultural values of your business opens the door for easy acceptance of new policies and legislative changes across the organization. Establishing how compliance is advantageous at each level of the company's structure will enable the employees to understand its importance more clearly. Also, you will need to identify the risk that compliance will avert in each strategic level of the business to back up your policy. Starting from the CEO to other company leaders and down to the temporary staff, everyone must understand why they should commit to transparency if the business risk-management efforts have to be effective.

- **Have a functional scope.** A compliance program should shift from a more retrospective role to a fast-forward preventive duty in a company (Euronext, 2024). The ability to foresee potential regulatory issues before they occur would mean an increased number of resources; thus, the scope of your strategy should include its implications. Although not all companies would be able to deploy an automated process or any artificial intelligence instantly during compliance development due to budgets, you'll need to consider it for you to achieve your goals.

- **Understand your regulatory environment.** The regulatory environment includes the legislation within your current location and the areas where your business extends. The best strategy for this step is to monitor draft bills when they are implemented, which can help you break down the requirements and procedures that can be provided to employees.

- **Develop formal policies and standards.** Once you understand regulatory obligations, you can now create procedures, policies, and standards required for complying with the law. Most of these policies may closely follow the technical standards laid out in the legislation. Still, considerations can also be made for adding internal checks to identify human and systematic errors before they become detrimental. Alternatively, you can liaise with regulators to help your business establish best practices regarding the regulations.

- **Train employees.** Thorough training on the required procedures is vital in ensuring that businesses are compliant and foster regulatory compliance growth. Employees should know how to identify, report, or escalate a compliance issue. Management must develop procedures for handling reports, detailing the necessary actions and how their dealings with business partners will be affected.

- **Accurate record-keeping is a must.** Several areas of legislation require accurate record-keeping of any activity within an organization, which is also a necessary area of compliance. For instance, some rules require that all records of insider information, suspicious reports, and disclosure delays be retained for five years. This legislation makes it essential to communicate all compliance rules to all employees because failure to do so will result in the company facing substantial financial penalties for incorrect record-keeping.

Training and Education

Compliance training is a vital component of developing a successful compliance program. Well-trained employees will understand their regulatory expectations and responsibilities, which can effectively contribute to maintaining a compliance culture. However, critical considerations in employee compliance training include setting up training programs, keeping programs ongoing, and monitoring, evaluation, and awareness programs.

Tailored training setups involve developing programs that are streamlined to your company's compliance needs. They should cover internal policies, relevant regulations, procedures, and industry best practices. Training programs should also be customized to be an ongoing process that regularly provides fresh ways to reinforce key concepts, introduce new regulations, and address emerging compliance concerns. Remember to monitor the program's effectiveness through assessments, evaluations, and employee feedback.

Moreover, awareness programs on building a compliance culture throughout the organization should be created to ensure effective employee compliance education. Awareness campaigns, posters, newsletters, and other means of internal communication can increase awareness and encourage employees to ask questions, raise concerns, and seek guidance on compliance issues.

The global quest for regulatory activities has given rise to new challenges, as more is needed for a company to be compliant in its headquarters. Enforcement of compliance will require vigilance across all company groups, which makes it possible for a business to face conflicting compliance as it moves from one region to another. An effective compliance program can help you adjust to these demands and react appropriately to the differences.

CRISIS MANAGEMENT

In the volatile business world, crises are not "if" but "when." A crisis can strike any business, regardless of size or industry, at any time. The possibility of unforeseen events is inevitable, from product recalls to data breaches and natural disasters to public relations fiascos. Hence, the adage "hope for the best, prepare for the worst" is apt in business.

While no company can eliminate the risk of a crisis, a well-crafted crisis management plan can hamper its impact. Effective crisis management is an essential survival strategy for your business. This chapter will guide you in preparing for the unknown, transforming potential crises into opportunities for growth.

PREPARING FOR A CRISIS

Running a business in such a volatile world requires more than quick fixes; it demands careful preparation and deliberate strategy. Preparation is the bedrock of efficient crisis management. It involves anticipating possible threats, assessing their impact, and devising strategies to address them.

Let's assume a scenario where a promising tech startup, Innovatech, has just launched a revolutionary new gadget. The product receives rave reviews, and the company is on a high. But just as success seems imminent, Innovatech faces a major crisis: A critical flaw in their product begins causing injuries to users. The situation quickly escalates as news outlets pick up the story, and social media is flooded with complaints and backlash.

The first step is to acknowledge the issue. This might seem simple, but admitting that there is a problem is sometimes one of the hardest things for a company to do. Following this acknowledgment, Innovatech can provide clear, honest information about the flaw. They should explain what happened and share how they plan to resolve the issue. Transparency builds trust, which is essential to navigating this kind of crisis. In addition to communicating about the issue, Innovatech needs to offer solutions that serve the needs of the affected consumers. This could involve refunds, exchanges for a safe model, or free repairs. By showing customers that their safety is a priority, Innovatech builds goodwill.

To effectively manage such crises, companies need a proactive approach that includes the following key components: a crisis management plan, a crisis team, and communication strategies. So, let's start with the fundamentals of a crisis management plan.

DEVELOPING A COMPREHENSIVE CRISIS MANAGEMENT PLAN

A crisis management plan (CMP) is your business's lifeboat. It's a blueprint for action when the unexpected happens. It provides a clear roadmap for responding to various crisis scenarios, ensuring your team knows what to do when a crisis arises. This plan should be a living document, continuously updated and tested to guarantee its relevance. Here's how to build a strong CMP:

- **Identify potential crises.** The first step is to conduct a thorough risk assessment. Identify the types of crises your business might face. These could vary from natural disasters and cyberattacks to public relations disasters and legal issues. Likewise, engage key stakeholders across different departments to capture various scenarios. Evaluating these risks will help you prioritize and prepare well.
- **Assemble a crisis management team.** Designate a team responsible for managing crises. This team should include members from various departments, such as legal, PR, IT, HR, and operations, ensuring a well-rounded approach to handling different aspects of a crisis. Each member should have clearly defined roles and responsibilities.
- **Develop communication protocols.** Clear and consistent communication is vital during a crisis. Develop internal and external communication protocols, including who will speak to the media, how to disseminate information, and how to address employees' concerns. Moreover, always offer transparency and timely updates, as this helps to maintain trust and quell rumors.
- **Create response strategies.** Devise detailed response strategies for each identified crisis scenario. Outline specific actions to take, assign responsibilities, and establish timelines. Include checklists and flowcharts to simplify the decision-making process during a crisis. Furthermore, allocate resources and collaborate with external parties, such as legal advisors and public relations experts.

- **Conduct regular training and drills.** Train your crisis management team and employees on the crisis management plan. Conduct mock drills to simulate different crisis scenarios, allowing your team to practice their response and identify areas for improvement.
- **Monitor and review.** Monitor potential risks and review your crisis management plan. Update it regularly to reflect changes in your business environment, new risks, and lessons learned from past crises.

ASSEMBLING A DEDICATED CRISIS MANAGEMENT TEAM

A crisis management plan is only as effective as the team executing it. Assembling a dedicated crisis team ensures that your company can respond swiftly and effectively, minimizing damage and steering the organization back on course. This team should consist of individuals with diverse skills and expertise, including:

- **Crisis Manager:** The leader of the CMT, responsible for coordinating the overall response and making strategic decisions.
- **Communications Specialist:** Managed internal and external communications, including media relations and stakeholder updates.
- **Legal Advisor:** Provides legal guidance and ensures the response complies with regulations and laws.
- **Operations Manager:** Oversees operational aspects of the response, including resource allocation and logistics.
- **IT Specialist:** Handles technology-related issues like data breaches or system failures.

PREPARING COMMUNICATION STRATEGIES FOR VARIOUS STAKEHOLDERS

Effective communication is the lifeblood of crisis management. How a company communicates during a crisis can influence its reputation, customer loyalty, and overall business success. A well-composed communication strategy involves customizing messages to different audiences, maintaining consistency, and responding promptly.

Understanding Your Audience

Before creating any message, you'll need to identify and understand your key stakeholders. This includes employees, customers, investors, media, the public, and government agencies. Each group has its own unique concerns and expectations. For instance, employees need to feel informed and supported. On the other hand, customers want to know that their safety and interests are prioritized, and investors seek transparency about the financial impact. Meanwhile, the media, always on the lookout for a story, must be managed carefully.

Crafting Your Message

The message you deliver should be clear, consistent, and honest. It should acknowledge the crisis, express empathy, and outline the steps to address the situation. Avoid jargon, technical terms, or evasive language. Here's how to develop your message based on the target audience:

- **Employees:** Focus on safety, support, and the company's commitment to them.

- **Customers:** Emphasize steps taken to resolve the issue, compensation (if applicable), and customer service channels.
- **Investors:** Provide transparent information about the financial impact, strategies incorporated to curb losses, and the company's long-term outlook.
- **Media:** Develop key messages, appoint a spokesperson, and be prepared to answer tough questions.
- **Community:** Demonstrate your commitment to the community, highlight any steps to rectify the situation, and express gratitude for their support.

Leveraging Multiple Channels

In today's digital age, information spreads fast. Using multiple channels to communicate your message and reach a wide audience is important. Note that each channel has strengths and weaknesses, and using several channels can help ensure the message reaches the target audience. These channels include press releases, social media, company websites, email, and traditional media outlets. Ensure you choose channels based on audience preferences and the nature of the crisis. For example, you can use social media to reach younger audiences and traditional media for older demographics. During a major crisis, you may need to give investors firsthand information about the situation to reinforce the organization's credibility and dispel rumors.

Maintaining Open Communication

A crisis often creates an information vacuum. Thus, rumors and speculation can quickly fill that void. To prevent misinformation from spreading, you need to maintain open communication channels and prepare employees to handle media inquiries and public interactions.

Building Trust

Trust is the cornerstone of any successful crisis response. You can rebuild trust with your stakeholders by being transparent, honest, and empathetic. Develop a long-term strategy to protect and enhance the brand. Moreover, a thorough after-action review should be conducted to identify lessons learned and steps to prevent crises from happening again.

Measuring and Adapting

Crisis communication is an ongoing process. Monitoring public sentiment, media coverage, and social media conversations is essential to identifying probable issues and modifying your message. In addition, gather input from stakeholders to assess communication effectiveness. Use insights to strengthen future crisis management efforts.

RESPONDING TO A CRISIS

The first few hours of a crisis are critical. Hence, every minute counts. A swift, decisive response can reduce damage and prevent escalating situations. Think of it as putting out a fire before it spreads. The faster you act, the better the outcome.

Immediate Actions: Taking Immediate Steps to Contain the Crisis

Imagine a tech company facing a data breach that exposes sensitive customer information. The first step in their response should be to secure their systems and prevent further unauthorized access. This might involve shutting down affected networks, isolating compromised data, and engaging cybersecurity experts. At the same time, they should begin evaluating the extent of the breach to understand what information was exposed and who may be affected.

In your response strategy, prioritize:

- **Containment:** Quickly assess the situation and implement measures to prevent the issue from worsening. For example, if there's a product recall due to safety concerns, halt sales and distribution immediately.
- **Assessment:** Gather facts about the crisis to understand its scope and impact. This might involve working with experts to analyze the situation thoroughly.
- **Response plan activation:** Put your crisis management plan into action. This plan should outline specific actions, assign responsibilities, and establish communication channels.
- **Stakeholder communication:** Inform key stakeholders about the crisis and the steps being taken to address it. This helps to maintain trust and transparency.

Internal Communication: Keeping Employees Informed and Engaged

In times of crisis, your employees are your frontline allies. Keeping them informed and engaged is vital for maintaining morale and promoting a unified response. For the tech company that experienced a data breach, employees are expected to be worried about their jobs and the company's future. In a situation like that, you'll need timely and transparent communication to help alleviate worries and help them stay focused and committed. Here's how to keep employees abreast of the recent happenings in the company:

- **Practice transparency.** Provide clear and honest updates about the situation. This helps to build trust and reduce speculation and misinformation.
- **Give regular updates.** Keep employees informed with frequent updates. Consistent communication helps manage anxiety and keeps everyone focused.
- **Provide support systems.** Offer support through counseling services or dedicated helplines. Crises can be stressful, and supporting your employees shows that you care about their well-being.
- **Encourage engagement.** Encourage employees to share their concerns and suggestions. Engaged employees are more likely to contribute positively to resolving the crisis.

External Communication: Managing Public and Media Relations Effectively

How you handle external communication during a crisis can influence your company's reputation and customer trust. Transparency and honesty are paramount when dealing with the media, customers, and the general public.

Consider a consumer goods company facing backlash over a defective product. How they communicate with the public can reduce or exacerbate the damage. To manage the public while saving the image of the company entails the following:

- **Develop key messages:** Key messages should be developed to address the core issues and communicate the company's position. These messages should be aligned with the company's values and be easily understandable to the public. In addition, ensure these messages are consistent across all platforms to prevent mixed messages, which can cause confusion and undermine trust.

- **Appoint a spokesperson:** Identifying a credible and articulate spokesperson is crucial for managing media inquiries. The spokesperson should be knowledgeable about the crisis and able to deliver the key messages effectively.
- **Proactive media engagement:** A proactive approach to media relations is essential. This involves contacting key media outlets to provide information and updates about the crisis. The goal is to control the narrative and prevent misinformation from spreading.

A Case Study of Greenleaf Organics

Background

Greenleaf Organics, a thriving midsized company specializing in organic food products, had built a loyal customer base with its commitment to quality and sustainability. The company was experiencing rapid growth, expanding its product lines and market reach. However, amid its success, Greenleaf faced an unforeseen crisis that tested its mettle and crisis management preparedness.

The Crisis

One summer, Greenleaf Organics released a new line of organic smoothies that soon became popular. Unfortunately, several customers reported severe allergic reactions after consuming the smoothies within weeks of the launch. Social media buzzed with complaints, and news outlets began covering the story, causing a significant public relations nightmare.

Initial Response

Greenleaf's management team quickly convened a crisis meeting. They activated their crisis management plan, which had been meticulously prepared and updated. The COO led the crisis management team, including PR, legal, quality control, and customer service representatives.

Communication Strategy

The first step was to address public concerns. Greenleaf issued a public apology and an immediate product recall, leveraging their pre-approved communication protocols. They communicated the issue on their website, social media platforms, and through press releases, ensuring consistent and clear messaging.

Investigation and Resolution

Simultaneously, Greenleaf's quality-control team launched a thorough investigation to identify the cause of the allergic reactions. They discovered that a batch of ingredients from a new supplier had been contaminated with traces of a common allergen. Greenleaf immediately severed ties with the supplier and implemented stricter quality-control measures.

Internal Coordination

The HR department supported affected employees, while customer service handled refunds and addressed customer concerns with empathy and efficiency. Legal counsel prepared for possible lawsuits, ensuring that all actions taken were in compliance with regulatory requirements and aimed at minimizing legal repercussions.

Learning and Improvement

After the crisis was resolved, Greenleaf's crisis management team comprehensively reviewed their response. They identified areas for improvement, such as faster detection of product issues and more thorough supplier vetting processes. These insights were incorporated into their updated crisis management plan.

Outcome

Thanks to their proactive crisis management plan, Greenleaf Organics survived the crisis and restored customer trust through transparent communication and swift action. Their proactive approach allayed financial losses, preserved their brand reputation, and strengthened their operational resilience.

Crisis management is an essential component of any business strategy. Being prepared with a comprehensive crisis management plan, an agile crisis team, and effective communication strategies can make all the difference when the unexpected occurs. You can navigate crises and emerge stronger by acting swiftly, maintaining transparency, and supporting your employees and customers.

Ultimately, it's not just about weathering the storm; it's learning and improving from each experience. Every crisis presents an opportunity to refine your processes, enhance your resilience, and build a culture of preparedness and trust within your organization. While preparation is key, learning from past legal challenges can improve your organization's ability to resolve crises.

The next chapter will explore the importance of understanding legal risks and turning liabilities into competitive advantages. These lessons will help you avoid pitfalls and strengthen your legal and operational framework.

LEARNING FROM LEGAL CHALLENGES

Navigating the maze of legal issues can be challenging for business owners, but have you ever wondered how they can impact the success of your business? Keeping up with legal obligations is like sailing through relentless waves where the horizon is uncertain, and the focus direction quickly changes. However, these challenges are vital for the success of any business, and this chapter is aimed at demystifying some of the common legal issues seen in business through root cause analysis, extracting lessons from past incidents, and aiding you in building a compliance culture.

Every sector of a business in the market industry has its own set of legal demands, and so do its challenges. These legal challenges are shared among different businesses and can be cut across sectors and industries, including incorrect tax declaration, regulatory compliance, unsatisfied customers, trademark infringement, and more.

For every business owner, the complications of tax laws are enough to make one's head spin. Unfortunately, misinterpretation of these laws can result in serious legal consequences. Different tax structures can also affect businesses differently, from how much you own to the deductions you are eligible for. Thus, proper understanding, tax reporting, and compliance are vital for avoiding penalties. Moreover, understanding employment laws can be challenging for most businesses, especially when mistakes in these areas can violate workplace regulations and labor laws.

Whether it is processing employee agreements, understanding the intricacies of the Fair Labor Standard Act, or even staying updated with the continually evolving landscape of discrimination laws, companies often find themselves in a tight spot about these matters. Also, the Infringement of customers' data can lead companies to expensive legal battles because protecting the creative assets of your business is so crucial in a digital world like ours. Trademarks, patents, copyrights, and trade secrets are some of the intellectual properties that pose a daunting task in ensuring they are duly protected.

Regulatory compliance issues arise when a business does not adhere to various local, state, and federal obligations, including environmental laws, health standards, and industrial-specific laws. Noncompliance with regulatory bodies can lead to legal disputes, hefty penalties, and reputational damage that can close the business down. Contract laws, when breached, can result in a business winding up in litigation because they communicate the obligations of the parties involved.

ANALYZING PAST INCIDENTS

It is disturbing for a business owner to face an immediate threat like a warrant letter or a lawsuit. However, understanding the problem and addressing the root causes can help you manage legal issues effectively. Analyzing legal incidents will involve identifying the root cause of previous legal challenges, extracting valuable lessons from them, and implementing changes to prevent future occurrences.

Root Cause Analysis

Root cause analysis of any challenge would describe the wide range of techniques, approaches, and tools used to reveal the cause of a problem. However, getting to the root of a challenge can be a daunting task, requiring combining multiple indicators to uncover the underlying issue. Most companies use a less intensive approach by reviewing the list of observable legal challenges and treating them one after the other. However, easy fixes can only kick the ball down the road, and without resolving the root cause, there are possibilities that the problem will continue. Here are the five steps that can guide you when investigating the principal problem behind your observations;

1. **Conduct a system-wide gap assessment.** To get to the root of a problem in your company, you must open your whole system up for thorough scrutiny. Never assume the problem is confined to a particular manufacturing system, section, or process. Work as a team to collect enough evidence and draw conclusions based on what you can document.
2. **Understand that multiple root causes exist.** Often, companies can launch an investigation into a process only to stop at a point without uncovering the full extent of the problem. It is essential to understand the scope of the analysis, regardless of how much time, effort, and resources it takes.

3. **Identify the possible solutions.** While most observable problems stem from various underlying causes, the root causes may have several solutions. To find these solutions, take a step back and inventory the possible ways to handle the core problem.

4. **Be thorough in defining the problem.** Only by clearly and appropriately defining a problem can it be identified as its root cause. Use the present observation as the starting point to handle the real problem before setting out for further investigation.

5. **Visualize a path to the root.** Getting to the root entails examining the issue and tracing it back to its starting point. To find this path as you investigate internally, create a visual chart that can help you conceptualize the direction of the investigation as you progress.

Lessons Learned From Past Incidents

Legal disputes have existed since industrialization, even in an innovative and emerging world like ours. The most famous and viral legal disputes in recent years have involved trademark infringement, data theft, copyright violations, and intellectual property theft.

Conflicts over trademark rights are so common that companies stand out constantly to defend their intellectual property against threat or infringement. They are the legal disputes that most often make headlines, draw the public's attention, and set a rough pathway that shapes trademark laws, especially with the global nature of our world. One such case was the Black Bear Micro Roastery trademark infringement lawsuit, a small coffee roaster in New Hampshire that was sued by Starbucks. The trademark infringement lawsuit filed in 2000 claimed that using "Black Bear" in the company's name and items could cause customer confusion with Starbucks's iconic logo having a bear-like image.

Despite the significant difference in market presence, industry, and size, Starbucks argued that using the bear imagery by Black Bear Micro Roastery could reduce or tarnish their brand trademark (Tradermarkraft, 2024). The legal battle was settled, and Black Bear Micro Roastery agreed to adjust its brand name and marketing items to avoid further confusion. This case shows that large companies have the right resources to guard their trademark and can—and will—take legal action against smaller businesses. Also, disputes like those between the two companies mentioned above can arise even when it is clear that the business operates in different market sectors and has various target audiences.

Continuous Improvement

Developing and maintaining strong business practices to help your company avoid potential legal issues is vital for ensuring compliance and legal safety. Creating the proper habits for these practices will help you avoid costly mistakes, and here are the practices that will guide you:

Understand the Importance of Legal Protection

Your business can be vulnerable to fines, lawsuits, and reputation damage without proper legal protection. Conscious habits can save you from such costly mistakes. You can protect your business by educating yourself on legal obligations and implementing safety measures.

Good business routines should be sustained, such as regularly reviewing and updating legal compliance, creating a written code of conduct and ethics for your employees, establishing efficient contracts with suppliers or vendors, and maintaining accurate records.

Develop a Regular Review Schedule

Creating a regular schedule for reviewing your legal compliance is crucial because it ensures that you are up-to-date with alterations in laws and regulations that could impact your business. Set a routine of reviewing your policies, contracts, and business practices, either monthly or quarterly, to ensure that they align with the current industry regulations.

Reviewing your legal compliance and policies regularly and consistently allows you to quickly identify compliance concerns before they become legal issues. This practice will help you demonstrate to regulators how seriously you take legal obligations.

Establish a Firm Contract

One practice that can safeguard your business from legal action is having a strong, legally bound agreement with partners, vendors, and clients. These written documents are vital for clearly outlining responsibilities, clarifying expectations, and setting boundaries for all parties involved. By ensuring that these contracts are well drafted, thoroughly checked, and legally bonded, future legal disputes can be avoided

Written Code of Conduct and Ethics

Creating a written code of conduct and ethics serves as a guideline that explicitly outlines your employee's expectations, cultural values, and behavioral standards. It helps to enforce a positive work environment and ensure that everyone understands their boundaries of operations and responsibilities in those places.

Moreover, communicating your business values and employee expectations to your team will protect your business against employee misconduct and future legal concerns and will promote professionalism. Review and update these codes to ensure they remain relevant.

Maintenance of Accurate Records

Detailed and accurate record-keeping of your transactions, communication, and business activities will serve as evidence when facing any legal dispute targeting finances. Additionally, having an organized business record can save you time when auditing or providing it to regulatory authorities. Also, when implemented for record-keeping, physical filling or digital storage systems will ensure that all recorded information can be easily accessed and retrieved.

BUILDING A RESILIENT ORGANIZATION

Resilient businesses do not just bounce back from misfortune but are propelled forward. They can absorb the shock of disruption and turn it into opportunities that capture transformational, inclusive growth. Resilience is the tendency of a business to anticipate, respond, prepare, and adequately adapt to negative interruptions to maintain a smooth, continuous operation. These businesses have superior products, a management team with the right decision-making skills, and no competitive advantage.

However, cultivating such business resilience can be difficult, especially in recent times, when several disruptions are blowing away business leaders, business units, and frontline employees. Think of global concerns like the war in Ukraine, the decline in the general market, and the global pandemic capable of disrupting systems for businesses. The reality becomes that there is no lifespan for change or expiration for business resilience because there will always be uncertainty, constant changes, and a sudden push to develop outcomes.

Culture of Compliance

Compliance culture is the lifeline of a resilient business because it creates an environment that ensures compliance is not just another habit written in a handbook but a practice that should be inculcated in everyone's routine. It will form the basis for responsible behavior and ethical practices since it promotes a shared mindset that values accountability, integrity, and transparency.

Moreover, building a compliance culture will allow your business to avoid legal problems that can cost your company's reputation and stability. It will enhance collaboration, productivity, and teamwork through the ethical framework and clear guidelines it provides for employees to make informed decisions. Most importantly, it strengthens a company's reputation in the marketplace, as most partners and customers prefer to work with businesses that show ethical practices.

Since a strong compliance culture drives long-term success, it becomes essential that businesses develop strategies that benefit the company, employees, and stakeholders and allow them to thrive equally. Also, setting up a booming culture of compliance will begin with the leadership demonstrating their dedication to following the outlined due process. They regularly communicate expectations, the importance of compliance, and values through their actions.

Additionally, comprehensive training programs that cover the company's compliance policy, ethical standards, and critical regulations should be encouraged. The training should be streamlined to address different employee responsibilities, offering interactive sessions that promote practical application and understanding. Also, it is essential to implement a system for evaluating and monitoring compliance efforts in the company because it allows the business to quickly assess and audit the risk to identify areas for improvement.

Ongoing Training

The essence of business resilience lies in maintaining readiness for alterations, which require a proactive and adaptable process. Regardless of the company's structure, resilience is aimed at achieving the planned readiness of its employees and stakeholders to keep up with market disruptions and technological advancements. This preparation to adapt and become stronger goes beyond risk management strategy; it is empowerment derived from continuous training and learning.

Companies that view training and prioritize continuous learning as a checkbox exercise have created a vigorous ecosystem where employees thrive and businesses succeed. An example of such resilience is Amazon, which embraced e-commerce by investing in cloud computing when it faced retail disruption.

Moreover, a resilient business would invest in learning to equip employees with the necessary skills, mindset, and knowledge to overcome challenges. These trainings are tailored to specific needs and emphasize developing a growth mindset, building adaptable skills, and creating a learning culture.

In building adaptable skills, learning programs are conducted to imbibe transferable skills such as critical thinking, collaboration, communication, and problem-solving in employees, enabling them to adapt to new situations (Ajoonu, 2024). Employees are also trained to leverage technology efficiently, which prepares them for potential disruptions. Also, employee education can promote a growth mindset, encouraging continuous learning and smooth transitions.

However, resilience training demands leaders who can make sound decisions in sudden, disruptive situations and communicate effectively during crises. Continuous training can ensure a pipeline of capable future leaders, which prepares the company for unforeseen circumstances. Additionally, building a culture of learning will build collective resilience through mentorship programs and collaborative learning participation.

Leadership Commitment

Ethical leadership's critical role in creating cultural integrity in a complex business environment must be considered. It goes beyond just complying with the law; it further encompasses setting the pace at the top by demonstrating a commitment to ethical behaviors. These ethical habits include:

Accountability

One of the key habits of ethical leadership is accountability. Ethical leaders are answerable not just to themselves but also to their teams. This means that when a mistake happens—whether it's a financial error or a breach of trust—these leaders take responsibility for their actions. They do not shift the blame onto their employees or external factors. Instead, they openly acknowledge the situation and work collaboratively with their teams to find solutions. For instance, if a project does not go as planned, an accountable leader would discuss what went wrong and how they can improve in the future, rather than punishing team members. This approach builds trust and encourages a culture where employees feel responsible for their actions and motivated to maintain ethical standards.

Fairness

Fairness is another essential component of ethical leadership. Leaders must ensure that decisions are made based on objective criteria rather than personal bias. This means treating every employee with respect and giving everyone an equal opportunity to contribute and succeed. For example, when assigning projects or promoting employees, ethical leaders should utilize clear criteria to guide their decisions. They may conduct performance reviews based on measurable outcomes rather than personal relationships. When employees see that they are treated fairly, they are more likely to feel valued and committed to their work.

Social Responsibility

Social responsibility is a fundamental aspect of ethical leadership. Leaders must consider the broader impact of their decisions, beyond just making a profit. This includes thinking about how their business affects employees, the community, and the environment. For example, if a company decides to cut costs by reducing employee benefits, ethical leaders will weigh this option against the potential negative impact on employee morale and turnover. They need to understand that long-term success often comes from investing in their workforce and being a good corporate citizen. When leaders align their business strategies with social responsibility, they create a positive work culture that resonates with employees and stakeholders alike.

So many things in a business can legally go wrong, and most of the challenges can affect your business reputation, relationships, finances, and time—and might cost you the business. Companies must learn, understand, and adopt strategies for avoiding common legal lapses to ensure sustainable growth. However, aside from legal challenges, inefficiency in protecting the privacy and details of your customers can adversely affect your business. The next chapter will help you understand data protection laws, how to implement data protection measures, and how to effectively manage data breaches.

DATA PROTECTION AND PRIVACY

A solid customer base is crucial for any business's prosperity, akin to how oxygen supports human life. Customer data offers significant benefits as companies examine this information for various purposes, such as enhancing user experience and gathering feedback.

Previously, organizations viewed data as their property despite being derived from customers' private actions. However, many countries recognize personal data as an individual asset entrusted to businesses. Companies that leverage personal data have transformed their collection, sharing, protection, and monetization methods.

The ideas elaborated in this chapter shed light on the regulations that govern data protection and the tactics available to counter security threats.

UNDERSTANDING DATA PROTECTION LAWS

In 2021, Amazon was fined $886.6 million for violating data protection laws (Leggett, 2021). Several other mega companies have been sanctioned for the same reason. This shows that data protection laws must be adhered to if a business is to thrive. However, understanding these laws can be cumbersome—they are specific to countries and states in the US.

Some of the widely used data protection laws are outlined below:

General Data Protection Regulation (GDPR)

The GDPR is the European Union (EU) data privacy law. It covers the data of EU citizens anywhere in the world, which means companies globally have to comply or face heavy fines.

Public and private bodies operating within the EU are subject to stipulations of the GDPR concerning personal data usage. This law imposes strict data requirements on organizations, mandating them to provide insights into how they utilize personal information.

Companies that violate this law risk being fined €20 million or 4% of their global revenue (whichever is greater). In addition, consumers have the right to seek compensation for damages.

Provisions of the GDPR

The GDPR grants users certain rights and imposes some obligations on businesses.

- **Consumers:** The GDPR offers consumers the right to consent to data collection, access their data, and ask for the rectification of their data.

- **Businesses:** The GDPR stipulates that companies must process accurate personal data transparently and use the data for legitimate purposes stated to the customer at the point of collection. The company is also responsible for demonstrating GDPR compliance.

California Consumer Privacy Act (CCPA)

This law permits any consumer in California to request access to all the data a business has on them and a comprehensive list of all the third parties with whom that data has been shared. In addition, the law allows consumers to sue companies if privacy guidelines are violated.

This law applies to businesses that service California residents and have at least $25 million in annual revenue. In addition, companies that have personal data on at least 50,000 Californians or generate a substantial part of their revenue from the data of Californian residents must comply with the law.

Provisions of the CCPA

The CCPA gives consumers rights and mandates certain obligations on businesses, service providers, and third parties.

- **The consumer:** Consumers have the right not to be discriminated against for asserting their rights and to initiate a private cause of action for data breaches. They also have the right to request the deletion of their personal information.
- **The business:** Companies must inform consumers of their rights, attend to their consumers' petitions, and employ impermeable security systems.

- **The service providers:** Service providers gather and process personal data on behalf of a business under legal terms. The CCPA mandates them to follow the terms of the agreement with a company and implement security safeguards.
- **Third parties:** Under the CCPA, third parties are expected to use personal information consistent with an agreement made with a business, notify users of updates concerning their practices, and give consumers the option of opting out.

Penalties of the CCPA

Businesses that are noncompliant with the CCPA risk civil penalties worth $7,500. When a consumer reports a data breach, the consumer may recover statutory damages of up to $750 or seek an injunctive deal and any nonmonetary relief the court deems appropriate.

Other Data Protection Laws

Data protection laws are specific to each country/state. Some of the prevalent data protection laws include:

- **Personal Information Protection and Electronic Documents Act (PIPEDA):** This law sets ground rules for private organizations that utilize personal information in Canada.
- **Digital Personal Data Protection Act (DPDPA):** This legislation regulates how businesses use personal data pertaining to Indian citizens.

Under this law, users have the right to have a say over how their data is used and file for privacy violations.

Industry-Specific Regulations

Several data protection laws are specific to certain industries, some of which include:

Financial Companies

The financial services industry is one of the most targeted industries for cyber-attacks. Financial institutions like banks and investment firms handle considerable personal and financial data. They also control very sensitive data, which, if compromised, can endanger customers and the company itself.

Some of the financial data protection laws include:

- **The Gramm-Leach-Bliley Act (GLBA):** This law requires companies that offer financial services such as loans, financial advice, or insurance to protect sensitive data and explain how they use customer data. It mandates that these firms inform their consumers as to how their data is being processed and the rights such customers have over their data.
- **The Payment Card Industry Data Security Standard (PCI-DSS):** This regulation focuses on companies that use credit card information. This law aims to secure cardholders' data, reducing the risk of data breaches and fraudulent activities. This statute results from the joint effort of well-known credit card companies such as Visa, American Express, and MasterCard.

Media Companies and COPPA

Apart from complying with the data protection laws of their state of operation, media companies such as streaming platforms and social media industries must comply with the Children's Online Privacy Protection Act (COPPA).

This law imposes specific requirements on operators of websites and online services to protect the privacy of children under 13. It specifies that sites must have verifiable parental consent before collecting or using any personal information of underage website users.

Such companies must keep children's data confidential and allow parents to access their children's data.

Due to COPPA's restriction on children's data collection, popular social media companies such as Facebook and X (formerly Twitter) require users to verify that they are age 13 or older when signing up on their platforms.

Health Companies and HIPAA

Health firms must comply with the Health Insurance Portability and Accountability Act (HIPAA) and federal data protection laws.

Under the provisions of HIPAA, patients have the right to access and correct their health information. Also, healthcare providers cannot use or share health information without the patient's consent.

IMPLEMENTING DATA PROTECTION MEASURES

Consumer data is extremely important and must be guarded at all costs. Data protection is a sequential process that involves sorting user data, implementing data security strategies, and setting up privacy policies.

Data Inventory

Customer data goes beyond names and emails. When customers interact with your business through social media engagement or browsing your website, you must fully comprehend the type of customer data you are gathering—it goes beyond names and emails. When customers interact with your business through social media engagement or browsing your website, you must fully comprehend the type of customer data you are gathering and how you can use it to the advantage of your business.

Types of Customer Data

Although customer data can be tagged in diverse forms, there are four main categories of customer data to look out for:

- **Basic data:** This refers to the primary information you gather from customers that classifies them as unique individuals. This data includes, but is not limited to, the name, email address, gender, phone number, date of birth, ethnicity, occupation, and social media handles of your customers.

   ○ Basic data can be obtained through newsletter subscriptions, account sign-ups, and purchases.

- **Engagement data:** This form of data refers to data that describes how your customers interact with your business. This data looks at your audience as a whole rather than individual persons.

- ○ Customer-engagement data includes website visits, ad engagements, and interaction on social media posts and emails.

- **Behavioral data:** Behavioral data is akin to engagement data, but it is more detailed. It gives insight into your customer's experience with your product or service.

  - ○ This includes purchase history, subscription renewals and cancellations, and users' time on your site.

- **Attitudinal data:** Attitudinal data helps you understand what customers think about your company. It comprises customer and client reviews, online survey responses, and one-on-one customer interactions.

Cataloging Consumer Data

Consumer data analysis requires a strategic approach. Businesses need the right tools to capture and analyze this data effectively, such as investing in efficient analytics platforms.

Compliance with legal frameworks is another critical aspect of handling user data. With regulations like GDPR and CCPA, businesses must ensure the collection and usage of consumer data conform to established laws.

Data Security

Cybersecurity is vital for protecting data from theft, loss, and corruption. Businesses must protect their data at all costs, be it delicate personal information or proprietary secrets.

Below are some practices that organizations can incorporate as part of their cybersecurity strategy:

Implement a Strong Cybersecurity Strategy

Developing a strategy that considers the welfare of employees and end users is imperative. Such an initiative must be all-encompassing and protect all types of data, particularly delicate information.

Revise Security Guidelines

Businesses must update security policies regularly as different sectors and processes adopt new technology and data-handling methods.

Run Security Updates and Backup Your Data

Most organizations accumulate vast amounts of data on customers and users. This requires a strategic approach when backing up data and managing those backups.

Employ Multi-Factor Authentication and Create Secure Passwords

Password requirements such as using uppercase and lowercase letters, symbols, and numbers are not strange to regular internet users. Interestingly, organizations have similar frameworks in place.

Multi-factor authentication is another popular technique that decreases the likelihood of fraudulent activity.

Monitor Third-Party Users and Applications

You can easily detect malicious activity and prevent breaches by controlling third-party activity, restricting access to sensitive information, and providing one-time passwords.

Adopt a Multifaceted Approach

The prevalence and sophistication of cybercrime have increased to the point where protecting your company today has to be approached from several angles. To effectively combat security threats, you will need proper technology, double authentication processes, verbal authentication on large monetary transfers, cyber insurance, and continuous improvement.

Train Your Employees

Employee training cannot be overemphasized when implementing proactive measures against cyber threats. Keeping your workers abreast of recent security practices will contribute to your organization's cybersecurity resilience.

Developing Transparent Privacy Policies

A good privacy policy gives your customers the confidence to purchase your products and ensures legal compliance with personal information protection laws.

- To develop transparent data privacy policies for your business, you must familiarize yourself with the data privacy laws that apply to your business, highlight the personal information to be collected, and explain how it will be used and secured. For example, if you collect credit card details, you can explain the encryption and security measures used to safeguard this sensitive data, which reassures users that their data is being managed responsibly and securely.
- You also need to explain how users can opt out and for how long you will retain data, as well as state the rights consumers have over their personal information.

- Providing contact information for users to ask questions is essential for maintaining transparency and trust.
- Users should have an accessible means of communication if they have any queries or apprehensions about using their data. You can include your business address in the privacy policy to increase your business's professional image and the trust of your users.

MANAGING DATA BREACHES

Suppose any personal data your business is responsible for goes missing, gets unduly altered, damaged, or disclosed to another party due to a cyberattack, theft, or other unforeseen circumstances. Such an incident is termed as a *personal data breach*.

Who would have thought ChatGPT, the well-known AI platform, would be in danger due to a mere bug? The tech platform reported its first data breach in 2023, which threatened bans from the mobile giant Samsung and the Italian government as sensitive user data was exposed (Pluralsight, 2023).

Therefore, it is extremely important to curb data breaches by all means to ensure the security of your business.

We will explore the possibilities of accomplishing this in the outlines below:.

Incident Response Plan

The first line of action is to develop a data breach response plan when a data breach occurs. This plan details the immediate action and information needed to manage the incident.

Though each plan is unique to each business, the steps below summarize the entirety of data breach plans:

1. **Properly understand the term "data breach".** As simple as it may sound, you need to understand the term "data breach" properly. A data breach is the movement of private information into a suspicious environment, which can manifest in any form. When that has happened, you are in an excellent position to employ various strategies to protect your business from security threats.
2. **Assess the risks and potential vulnerabilities in your business data.** Before developing a data breach response plan, carefully consider how each risk and vulnerability impacts your organization and its operations. Also, evaluate the risk of sensitive data reaching the wrong hands.
3. **Implement strategic processes.** It is advised to set up a response team and create policies that detect and contain the event while minimizing overall exposure of existing data to further damage. These processes include enacting secure password policies, using monitoring services, protecting against accidental data loss, and obtaining cyber insurance.
4. **Regularly review the data-breach response plan.** Once a data breach has been resolved, the plan must be evaluated to bridge any gaps discovered while mitigating the breach.

Complying With Legal Requirements for Breach Notifications

Regulatory-compliant data-breach notifications are essential to maintain trust and comply with legal requirements when a breach occurs. Notification laws pertaining to data breaches may differ based on jurisdiction, the type of data breach, and the number of records affected.

Data breach notifications are a vital component of a company's response strategy. They inform individuals whose personal data may have been compromised, helping them take necessary precautions to protect themselves from plausible harm.

However, notifying affected individuals is not as simple as sending a memo. Businesses must navigate a complex web of laws and regulations to ensure their notifications are compliant and effective.

Here are some key federal and state regulations that mandate data-breach notifications:

- **General Data Protection Regulation (GDPR):** This regulation mandates that businesses notify the breach within 72 hours of identifying it.
- **California Consumer Privacy Act (CCPA):** This law requires businesses to notify California residents of breaches involving their data within 45 days.
- **Health Insurance Portability and Accountability Act (HIPAA):** This act mandates that healthcare organizations notify individuals of breaches involving protected health information within 60 days.
- **Other state-specific laws:** Each state has specific notification requirements but generally requires notification within 30–60 days.

Post-Breach Actions

After a data breach, you can mitigate the damage by acting quickly, containing the breach, and launching the recovery process. Unfortunately, the whole breach mitigation and notification process takes a long time, and by the end, most of the damage would have been done.

The safest thing to do is to prevent a data breach from occurring in the first place. So, how do you make it happen?

Steps to Mitigate Damage and Prevent Future Breaches

1. **Restrict access.** Each person with access or potential access to data is another vulnerability. If 1,000 people log into a system with personal information, that represents 1,000 vulnerabilities; any individual in that group could be the weak link. If only 10 people can access that information, you will reduce the risk by 99%.
2. **Enhance overall security.** Data security is a vast and multifaceted topic, but techniques like enhanced systems, restriction, monitoring third-party activity, and simple routine checks and updates all sum up to boosting the security of your business.
3. **Train your employees.** It may surprise you that most data breaches do not result from one hell-bent hacker forcing his way past your seemingly infallible defense systems. Funny enough, many breaches are attributable to human errors that employees can often make. Therefore, training your employees on the best data security practices is crucial to your enterprise's prosperity.

In summary, no data security strategy can indefinitely guarantee protection against all potential threats. This is due to the ever-evolving nature of the digital landscape. It is essential to stay informed about relevant laws and regulations concerning data management and disposal. To effectively avert data breaches, ongoing evaluation of your security measures is imperative.

In today's dynamic business environment, adherence to environmental and social standards has become crucial for a company's success. Imagine operating a business that prioritizes ecological responsibility and community welfare. Such a commitment will attract reputable investors and enhance your organization's social standing.

The next chapter discusses how these elements subtly yet significantly influence a company's achievement.

ENVIRONMENTAL AND SOCIAL RESPONSIBILITY

Nowadays, businesses are constantly examined for how they perform financially and how they affect the environment and society. For every business owner, now is the right time to welcome more environmental and social responsibilities, mainly because consumers and stakeholders are becoming more aware of corporate behavior. Apart from boosting the image of your company or encouraging more customer dedication, it can serve as a strong defense against lawsuits. Once a business owner can actively manage environmental and social issues, they can reduce risks or avoid lawsuits and class actions. Let's look at some of these environmental and social responsibilities.

ENVIRONMENTAL COMPLIANCE

The first aspect of environmental compliance is understanding environmental laws and regulations. Once a business understands this, it can actively prevent itself from engaging in environmental litigation. Any form of legal threat can be expensive for a company. However, environmental litigation can also damage the image of such a company.

Some essential laws every business owner should know are the Clean Air Act, Clean Water Act, and the Emergency Planning and Community Right-to-Know Act (EPCRA). The Clean Air Act summarizes how businesses should discharge substances into the air and other substances that can cause air pollution. The Environmental Protection Agency (EPA) implements this act. Therefore, they have the right to fine and sanction any business that refuses to comply with the law.

The Clean Water Act was enacted in 1977 and updated in 1987. It tells companies how to use water bodies to reduce water pollution effectively. The EPA also implemented this act. At the same time, EPCRA mandates states to enforce a response plan in case of any emergency or occurrence that might result in environmental hazards for society and people. Every company needs to adhere to the rules of EPCRA, especially when informing people about possible risks.

There are still several environmental regulations and requirements, so every business owner should equip themselves with this knowledge by seeking assistance from legal professionals about how to navigate the environmental laws.

Sustainability Practices

Business owners sometimes need to realize the need to include sustainability practices. However, more companies currently accept the triple-bottom-line concept. That is, they understand that they can get profits from their business and at the same time get the required social and environmental benefits.

Once business owners realized this, a new business model, Corporate Social Responsibility (CSR), was incorporated. This also helps businesses focus on social and environmental responsibilities while focusing on their organizational goals. Any business that wishes to embrace sustainability practices can use various strategies. Here are some business practices you should implement.

Collaborate With Nonprofit Organizations

Several organizations that love to incorporate sustainability often fail to implement vital initiatives, probably because they need to learn how to do it, and it takes a long time to learn. However, the way to solve this problem, especially for businesses exposed to the world of sustainability practices, is to collaborate with nonprofits in any space they like. There are several nonprofits, and they often have the resources and expertise to help you. Even when they can't help you, they will help you enforce policies in your business that can positively impact you while adjusting to the world of sustainability. If your business is interested in labor issues, environmental concerns, or something different, there's a nonprofit that has almost the same goal as your company.

Train Your Employees

Most of the time, any business thriving in sustainability practices must train its employees about the issues and carry them along. What's the benefit? First, teaching your employees about sustainability practices can boost buy-in and reduce the chances that you'd go back to your former ways. Also, it enables your employees to do their best, which can go a long way in increasing their morale. How you train your employees about your business matters hinges greatly on the situation. This can be done by conducting webinar lectures or buying corporate social responsibility teachings.

Encourage Volunteerism

Another good way to carry your employees along in the sustainability process is to encourage volunteerism. There are several strategies you might utilize to achieve this objective. For instance, you can implement paid time off for employees who want to volunteer. It doesn't have to be much—even just giving your employees one or two days of VTO can go a long way in motivating them. Also, you can conduct a volunteer drive where your employees are encouraged to volunteer at local charities.

Environment Audits

An environmental audit is essential to review a company's environmental performance. It assists the management in noting environmental hazards and enforcing measures to reduce them. The importance of the audit is to emphasize the areas that should be worked on to show the company's dedication to sustainability. Environmental audits involve an all-inclusive review of a company's system of operation and its impact on the environment. They check if the business adheres to the environmental laws, check for potential hazards, and determine the efficiency of environmental management systems.

What are the essential things you should note about audits?

We have both internal and external auditors. The internal auditors are from the company's staff, while a third party conducts external audits. External auditors are stricter and carry out a proper scrutiny of the company's environmental performance.

Environmental audits include checking for potential air, water, or waste-disposal hazards. They also check the company's environmental policies to make sure they're adhering to regulations. Once these areas have been identified, businesses can create specific strategies and techniques to minimize their ecological impact and improve sustainability practices.

CORPORATE SOCIAL RESPONSIBILITY

Corporate Social Responsibility (CSR) refers to the steps and processes carried out by a company to impact society positively. It also refers to the moral and virtuous standard, which is more than just state laws and regulations; it is voluntary work and willingness to contribute to the good of society. CSR involves business procedures created to improve rather than demean society, considering how these can affect the workers, the environment, and other aspects of life.

Why Should a Business Carry Out CSR?

When companies are concerned about more than profit enhancement and its positive impact on society, such businesses are also heaping treasures for themselves. Once the CSR strategy is carefully carried out, it gives the company an edge over the others. Ultimately, it can help businesses retain valuable employees, improve customer dedication, and boost their image.

How Can You Accomplish CSR in Your Business?

Before you look into CSR, you should understand the concept of CSR and how your business can adequately adjust to it. Once this has been done, there are some valuable steps you can use to blend it into your business, which will be discussed next.

Determine and Review Industry Issues

First, before you begin, identify your industry's issues. Before a social impact program can offer the correct value to society, workers, customers, or even stakeholders, it must align with the company's specific area of competence. Develop tactics around your strengths, goals, and knowledge, and pay more attention to particular issues that align with your expertise.

Have a Solution

After identifying the issues, the next step is to know precisely how your company can help address the matter. Once you can define this, you can evaluate the value proposal of your CSR efforts. Utilize this chance effectively to be creative and show the world how good your company is.

Strengths

The next step is to create a detailed plan on how you wish to address the matter. Have a vision that will keep you firing throughout, and involve others in every decision you make. Reach out to customers and your workers for their feedback. Also, conduct an audit of your resources and then gather all the information to make a concise and intelligent plan.

Communicate With Others

If you want to enjoy the benefits of CSR, then your plans need to include an effective communication strategy. Once you communicate honestly, you can earn others' trust in your business and provide a good working environment for your employees.

Implement and Monitor the Plan

Lastly, execute your plan and determine whether it's improving society. Ensure you constantly review your goals and note what works and the changes that need to be made.

Due to the increasing demand for responsibility, every business should be actively involved in CSRs. What a company does affects society's condition regarding job vacancies, health, human rights, and education. Once you can adhere to these steps, you can set up a team to help carry out creative strategies that benefit all aspects of society and pave the way for a better future.

As more businesses realize the need to play a part in the welfare of society and the environment, CSR has become a leading trend. At the center of CSR, we have stakeholder engagement that helps implement an inclusive approach to developing society.

Stakeholder Engagement

Stakeholder engagement is interconnected to CSR, so let's see why it's essential:

- **Know what stakeholders need:** Interacting with stakeholders helps businesses understand the needs, cares, and expectations of various stakeholder groups, thereby ensuring congruence between CSR initiatives and stakeholder priorities.
- **Ensuring trust and lawfulness:** As a business owner, once you include stakeholders, you can build honesty and accountability, which can bring about trust and boost your business's image among the stakeholders.
- **Cooperation and co-creation:** Stakeholder engagement is more than just seeking help from time to time; it involves working together to create strategies and using

stakeholder professionalism and resources to achieve the desired results.

- **Reduces risk:** A proactive stakeholder engagement helps businesses identify possible threats and problems related to CSR activities. It also allows for the implementation of helpful tactics to mitigate adverse effects on the industry and stakeholders.
- **Improves decision-making:** Involving stakeholders brings different perspectives, ideas, and expertise that can lead to better decisions for the business. Also, it helps to make the right decisions that align with what the stakeholders want.
- **Credibility and reporting:** Another critical aspect of stakeholder engagement is that it helps businesses to be credible for their CSR allegiance by fostering honest reporting on CSR advancements and results. This helps to encourage trust among the stakeholders.

Communicating CSR Efforts and Results

You need to communicate CSR efforts and results to ensure the public knows how your business carries out its social responsibilities. You can use several methods, such as press meetings, social media, or advertisements, to help you convey CSR in an organized manner. Here's a little tool to help you:

Identify Your Goals

One potent way to communicate CSR is to show how your company's goals align with its CSR practices. For example, Ben and Jerry's backed up their goal by creatively adding value to society. They achieved this by giving out considerable grants to nonprofit organizations tackling poverty. Assisting in fighting poverty is a good way of helping society, and the grant program is based on the organization's values. You can examine how Starbucks or Ben and Jerry's have achieved perfect CSR messaging and apply it to your business.

Be Bold

Adopting a courageous approach is essential to effectively convey CSR. Issues such as climate change and racial injustice weigh heavily on consumers' minds and can influence their buying decisions. As public consciousness regarding environmental sustainability and social responsibility grows, every business leader must actively implement strategies that bring about meaningful change within their communities.

COMMUNITY RELATIONS

Every business should learn to interact with its community by establishing and maintaining trust with local communities, developing programs that benefit the company, and handling conflicts with community stakeholders. Your community group can provide insights that can bring innovative and splendid ideas. So, how can your business interact with its community and benefit from them?

Be Open to Communication

While forming a relationship with the whole community, you must always be open to welcoming communication between leaders and community members. This means that you're constantly arranging meetings and habitual round-table conversations. You can also set up a forum for community members to allay their fears and questions. It would help if you also carried the community along with any significant decision being made within your company; such decisions should be passed right away before it's implemented. Once the community members feel heard and cared for, they feel loved and more motivated to support your business and decisions. Furthermore, you should be open to accepting feedback regularly and be responsive to what the community members and leaders say to ensure smooth operation.

Give Room for Community Participation

Some companies make decisions without involving their clients or consumers. However, if you want to create a tighter bond with your community, you should invite people with close affiliations with the community. You can organize outdoor or round-table meetings where everyone can be free to participate without any form of limitation. Please note that you don't have to hold such meetings regularly, but they should be consistent. It would help if you carried the community along with major decisions being made, and any later agreed-upon decision should be passed across to them with the underlying reasons behind them. When communicating, use simple and direct language that everyone understands, and avoid using professional jargon.

Form a Bond With Community Leaders

If you want to build community trust, you can achieve that by forming a bond with the community leaders. These leaders include youth leaders, religious leaders, educational leaders, and so on. Once you can develop a healthy relationship with them, they can then assist you in achieving your goals. They will also help you to understand the concept of community culture. Once these leaders approve of your business, they can serve as a platform to make your intentions known throughout the community. It's important to note that community relations have a foundation in leadership, and sometimes, the only way to move forward is with the approval of leaders in the community.

In summary, as a business owner, you can avoid lawsuits by paying more attention to environmental and social responsibilities. Once you can carry out sustainability practices, reduce the negative environmental impact, and treat your employees and the community correctly, you can build trust and avoid any form of legal threat. Also note that honesty, adherence to regulatory requirements, and stakeholder engagement not only boost the image of your company but also help create a flexible business model that appropriately deals with potential lawsuits and class actions.

PAY IT FORWARD!

Every challenge you face will help you to grow—but when it comes to legal matters, this can only happen when you have a firm knowledge base to draw on. Now that you do, you're in the perfect position to help other businesses out.

Simply by sharing your honest opinion of this book and a little about what you've learned here, you'll help more business owners connect with it, and that could make a huge difference to their success.

LEAVE A REVIEW!

Thank you so much for your support. May your business go from strength to strength!

Scan the QR code below

CONCLUSION

Maintaining caution, preparedness, and proactivity is crucial for achieving success in an environment where legal challenges can emerge unexpectedly. This book explored the intricacies of legal risk management, providing you with essential insights and strategies to protect your organization from potential lawsuits and class-action suits.

You have gained insights into the legal landscape and recognized the significance of thorough policies to mitigate potential threats. You now possess the ability to identify risks early and intervene effectively, ensuring your organization operates smoothly while safeguarding its reputation and finances.

The discussions on hiring practices, product quality, and contract management have underscored the necessity of establishing clear guidelines and efficient processes. You can circumvent legal challenges by building a supportive work environment, prioritizing product safety, and effectively managing contracts while enhancing customer satisfaction and efficiency.

Protecting your intellectual property, adhering to regulations, and ensuring data security are now integral to a successful business strategy. By grasping and implementing the insights shared in these chapters, your organization can excel in compliance and innovation, confidently working within all these intricate rules and regulations.

Drawing lessons from previous legal encounters is vital for building resilience. Preparing for unforeseen events and continually refining your approaches will strengthen your organization during difficult times. A dedication to a culture of compliance and accountability begins at the executive level, ensuring that all team members appreciate the significance of legal standards in their everyday responsibilities.

Ultimately, demonstrating accountability toward the environment and society is imperative. By integrating sustainable practices and actively participating within your community, you safeguard your business and contribute positively to society.

As you conclude this book, remember to embrace each challenge as an opportunity for growth, and commit to enhancing your legal practices. You are now armed with invaluable insights and actionable strategies to propel your organization toward success. Cheers to your business success!

Running a business amid so many legal requirements may appear daunting, but with the knowledge you've acquired, you are prepared to confront these challenges head-on. Your business can flourish in a legally sound environment by prioritizing prevention, nurturing a responsible culture, and embracing transformation. Here's to a future where your organization not only endures but thrives, free from lawsuits and firmly rooted in compliance and integrity!

APPENDIX I: SELF-ASSESSMENT QUIZZES

In the business landscape, evaluating various aspects of your company is crucial to avoid legal complications. One effective method for conducting this evaluation is through self-assessment quizzes. These quizzes are designed to help you scrutinize practices that could expose your organization to risk.

By exploring the key areas highlighted in these quizzes, you can take proactive steps to protect your business from potential legal issues.

Quiz 1: Advertising Practices

This quiz focuses on the advertising practices of your business, which play a significant role in how customers perceive your brand. By examining your advertising materials, disclaimers, and potential complaints, you can ensure that your marketing strategies comply with legal regulations. Assessing these elements enables you to build consumer trust while minimizing the risk of misleading advertising claims.

Have you reviewed your advertising materials for legal compliance?

☐ Yes

☐ No

Do you use disclaimers to clarify claims made in your advertisements?

☐ Yes

☐ No

Have you ever received a complaint about misleading advertising?

☐ Yes

☐ No

Are your marketing strategies regularly assessed for legal risks?

☐ Yes

☐ No

Quiz 2: Employee Practices

This quiz evaluates how well your business supports and protects its workforce. By reviewing your employee handbook, training programs, and grievance processes, you can identify areas for improvement in maintaining a healthy workplace environment. This self-assessment is vital for ensuring employee satisfaction and meeting legal obligations regarding workplace behavior.

Do you have a written employee handbook that outlines workplace policies?

☐ Yes

☐ No

Are your employees regularly trained on topics such as harassment and discrimination?

☐ Yes

☐ No

Do you have a clear process for addressing employee grievances?

☐ Yes

☐ No

Have you conducted an anonymous survey to gauge employee satisfaction and safety concerns?

☐ Yes

☐ No

Quiz 3: Contracts and Agreements

Contracts and agreements are foundational to business operations, and this quiz encourages you to assess your current practices in this area. By ensuring you use written contracts and have them reviewed legally, you can clarify responsibilities and expectations in all significant transactions. Evaluating these aspects helps mitigate potential disputes and strengthens your business relationships.

Do you use written contracts for all significant business transactions?

☐ Yes

☐ No

Have all contracts been reviewed by a legal professional before signing?

☐ Yes

☐ No

Are your contracts clear and specific in outlining responsibilities and expectations?

☐ Yes

☐ No

Do you have a process for updating contracts regularly to reflect changes in business practices?

☐ Yes

☐ No

Quiz 4: Compliance and Regulations

Staying compliant with industry regulations is critical for the success of your business. This quiz prompts you to evaluate your awareness of these regulations, the appointment of a compliance officer, and ongoing updates relevant to your legal obligations. A strong compliance framework not only protects your business from legal repercussions but also enhances your reputation within your industry.

Are you aware of the regulations specific to your industry?

☐ Yes

☐ No

Do you have a compliance officer or appointed person responsible for legal matters?

☐ Yes

☐ No

Are you subscribed to legal updates relevant to your business?

☐ Yes

☐ No

Have you conducted a compliance audit in the past year?

☐ Yes

☐ No

Quiz 5: Risk Management Strategies

Effective risk management is essential to navigating the uncertainties of business operations. This quiz helps you assess whether you have a risk management plan in place and if your employees are educated on its importance. By regularly evaluating potential risks and consulting legal experts, you can reinforce your business's resilience against unexpected challenges.

Do you have a risk management plan in place?

☐ Yes

☐ No

Are employees trained on the importance of risk management?

☐ Yes

☐ No

Do you conduct regular assessments of potential risks within your business operations?

☐ Yes

☐ No

Have you consulted with a legal expert about your risk management practices?

☐ Yes

☐ No

* * *

Scoring Your Quizzes

- For each "Yes" answer, give yourself 1 point.
- For each "No" answer, give yourself 0 points.

Interpreting Your Score

- **0–5 points:** High risk—Consider immediate action to assess and improve your practices.
- **6–10 points:** Moderate risk—Focus on areas of improvement identified in your answers.
- **11–15 points:** Low risk—You are on the right track, but continue to monitor and update your practices.

APPENDIX II: WORKSHEETS

This set of worksheets is designed to help business owners systematically assess compliance, identify risks, create actionable plans for vulnerabilities, and ensure follow-up on necessary actions. By utilizing these worksheets, businesses can create a culture of compliance and proactively manage risks to enhance their operational integrity.

WORKSHEET 1: COMPLIANCE CHECK-UP

This worksheet is intended to help businesses evaluate their adherence to critical regulations and policies. By identifying areas of compliance, you can ensure that employee rights are protected, harassment is addressed, and privacy is maintained. Use this tool to assess the current state of your compliance practices and determine any necessary actions.

Business Name: _____

Date: _____

Contact Person: _____

Instructions: Use this worksheet to assess compliance with key regulations applicable to your business.

Compliance Area	Yes	No	Comments/Action Required
Are employee rights outlined in an employee handbook?			
Is there a process in place for reporting harassment?			
Do you train employees on compliance laws?			
Are privacy policies communicated to customers?			
Is there a designated compliance officer?			

Notes:

_____

_____

_____

WORKSHEET 2: RISK ASSESSMENT

The purpose of this worksheet is to help you identify and evaluate potential risks that could affect your business operations. By rating each risk and outlining mitigation strategies, you can proactively address vulnerabilities that could lead to critical failures.

This organized approach enables you to prioritize risks and assign responsibility for managing them effectively.

Business Name: _____

Date: _____

Contact Person: _____

Instructions: Use this worksheet to identify and assess potential risks in your business. Rate each risk on a scale of 1 (low) to 5 (high).

Risk Area	Description of Risk	Rating (1–5)	Mitigation Strategy	Responsible Person
Advertising Practices				
Employee Management				
Contractual Agreements				
Regulatory Compliance				
Customer Relations				

Notes:

_____

_____

_____

WORKSHEET 3: ACTION PLAN FOR VULNERABILITIES

This worksheet is designed to facilitate the creation of actionable plans based on the vulnerabilities identified in your compliance check-up and risk assessment. By detailing specific actions, deadlines, and responsible individuals, you can ensure accountability and track progress in addressing areas of concern.

Business Name: _____

Date: _____

Contact Person: _____

Instructions: Use this worksheet to create an actionable plan based on vulnerabilities identified in your compliance check-up and risk assessment.

Vulnerability	Action Required	Deadline	Responsible Person	Status

Notes:

_____

_____

_____

WORKSHEET 4: FOLLOW-UP CHECKLIST

The follow-up checklist serves as a practical tool for monitoring the completion of action items from your action plan. By regularly reviewing the status of each action item, you can maintain focus on your compliance and risk management goals, ensuring that all necessary steps are taken to strengthen your business operations.

Business Name: _____

Date: _____

Contact Person: _____

Instructions: Use this checklist to follow up on the action items from your action plan.

Action Item	Completed (Yes/No)	Comments	Follow-Up Date

Notes:

_____

_____

_____

WORKSHEET 5: TRAINING NEEDS ASSESSMENT

This worksheet helps identify employee training needs to improve compliance and risk management practices. By assessing their employees' current skill levels and knowledge gaps, businesses can provide targeted training to their staff.

Business Name: _____

Date: _____

Contact Person: _____

Instructions: Use this checklist to follow up on the action items from your action plan.

Training Area	Current Skill Level (1–5)	Knowledge Gap	Suggested Training	Responsible Person
Compliance Regulations				
Workplace Safety				
Data Privacy				
Risk Management				
Customer Service				

Notes:

_____

_____

_____

WORKSHEET 6: INCIDENT REPORTING

This worksheet is designed to document any compliance or risk incidents that occur in the business. By recording these incidents, companies can analyze trends and improve their practices to minimize future occurrences.

Business Name: _____

Date: _____

Contact Person: _____

Instructions: Use this checklist to follow up on the action items from your action plan.

Incident Date	Description of Incident	Root Cause	Action Taken	Responsible Person

Notes:

_____

_____

_____

APPENDIX III: STEPS INVOLVED IN A LAWSUIT OR CLASS ACTION

A lawsuit or class action is a formal process in which one party seeks justice or compensation from another party. This process can seem complex, but breaking it down into steps can help clarify what happens. Each part of the legal process plays a crucial role, and understanding each phase makes the entire experience less intimidating.

Step 1: Initiation of the Legal Process

The first step in the legal process is *initiation*—when a person or group decides to file a lawsuit. They usually start by consulting a lawyer who specializes in the relevant area of law. It is essential for the client to discuss the details of the case openly. For instance, if someone is injured in an accident and believes someone else is liable, sharing all relevant facts with the lawyer is crucial.

After this discussion, the lawyer can help determine whether there is a valid cause of action. A cause of action is a legal reason to sue; it forms the foundation of the case. If the lawyer believes there is a strong case, they will draft a document called a *complaint*. The complaint outlines the plaintiff's allegations and the relief requested. In our example of the accident victim, the complaint may explain how the other party caused the accident and what damages the victim is seeking, such as medical expenses or lost wages.

Step 2: Serving the Defendant

Once the complaint is filed with the court, the next step is to serve the defendant. This means that a copy of the complaint and a document called a *summons* is formally delivered to the person or entity being sued. The summons informs the defendant that they are being sued and provides instructions on how to respond.

Properly serving the defendant is important, as it ensures that the defendant is aware of the lawsuit and has an opportunity to defend themselves. In some cases, if the defendant is not reachable, a judge may allow alternative methods of service. This ensures that the legal process can continue as required.

Step 3: The Defendant's Response

After being served, the defendant typically has a set period, usually around 30 days, to respond to the complaint. They can file an answer, which addresses the allegations made in the complaint. In the answer, the defendant can admit or deny each claim. For instance, if our accident victim alleges that the defendant ran a red light, the defendant might admit to running the red light but argue that it was still not their fault.

Alternatively, the defendant can also file a *motion to dismiss*—a request to the court to dismiss the case for various reasons, such as the claim being unsubstantiated or having no legal basis. If the court denies this motion, the defendant must proceed with their response.

Step 4: Discovery Phase

After the defendant has responded, the case moves into the *discovery phase*. This step is essential as both parties gather evidence to support their claims. Discovery includes things like interrogatories (written questions that the other party must answer), requests for documents, and depositions (out-of-court interviews under oath).

For example, the accident victim might request documents related to the defendant's driving history or any previous accidents. The defendant might, in turn, ask for medical records related to the victim's injuries. This exchange of information is crucial as it helps both parties evaluate the strengths and weaknesses of their cases and prepares them for what's ahead.

Step 5: Pre-Trial Motions

Once discovery is complete, either party can file *pre-trial motions*. These motions can request the court to rule on specific issues before the trial begins. For instance, a party may ask the court to exclude certain pieces of evidence they believe are irrelevant or inadmissible.

These motions can significantly impact the trial. If the court grants a motion to exclude evidence, that evidence cannot be presented during the trial, which can change the outcome.

Step 6: Settlement Negotiations

Before the trial starts, many cases are resolved through settlement negotiations. During this phase, the parties discuss possible resolutions without going to court. This negotiation can happen informally or through mediation, where a neutral third party helps facilitate dialogue between the parties.

Settlements can save time and money for both sides. For example, in our accident case, if the defendant offers the plaintiff a sum of money to settle, the plaintiff can choose to accept it rather than wait for a potentially lengthy trial. Settlements allow parties to have more control over the outcome and can lead to quicker resolutions.

Step 7: The Trial

If the case does not settle, it proceeds to *trial*—when both parties present their evidence and arguments in front of a judge or a jury. The trial begins with opening statements, followed by witness testimonies and the presentation of evidence. Each side has an opportunity to cross-examine witnesses.

After all evidence is presented, closing arguments are made, summarizing the case's critical points. Finally, the judge or jury will deliberate and render a verdict. In our accident example, the jury will decide whether the defendant is liable for the plaintiff's injuries and, if so, what damages—how much money—should be awarded.

Post-Trial Motions

After a verdict is reached, parties might file *post-trial motions*. This can include motions for a new trial or motions to amend the judgment. For instance, if new evidence emerges after the trial that a party believes could significantly change the case's outcome, they could request a new trial.

These motions can prolong the resolution of a case, as courts must consider the requests before finalizing everything.

Appeal Process

If one party is dissatisfied with the trial's outcome, they can choose to *appeal* the decision. An appeal is the process of asking a higher court to review the lower court's decision. This does not mean the case is retried; rather, the appeal looks for legal errors that may have affected the verdict.

The appealing party submits a *brief* outlining their reasons for the appeal, while the other party can file a response. The appellate court reviews the materials presented, and often, the decision from the appellate court is final, although further appeals to higher courts do sometimes occur.

Resolution

Ultimately, the legal process leads to resolution, whether it comes from a trial verdict or a settlement. The litigation process can be lengthy, often taking months or even years, but navigating each step carefully can lead to fair outcomes for all parties involved.

Understanding the legal process serves as an essential tool for those engaging with the system. Each phase is intricately connected, reflecting the complexities of law and justice. Familiarity with these steps can also alleviate stress and bring about informed decisions throughout the entire legal journey.

REFERENCES

Ajoonu, P. (2024, June 26). *Building organisational resilience: The critical role of continuous learning & development*. Businessday NG. https://businessday.ng/opinion/article/building-organisational-resilience-the-critical-role-of-continuous-learning-development/

Ajoonu, P. (2024, June 26). *Building organisational resilience: The critical role of continuous learning & development*. Businessday NG. https://businessday.ng/opinion/article/building-organisational-resilience-the-critical-role-of-continuous-learning-development/

Art and Media Law. (2023, September 4). *Privacy and data protection in streaming law*. Art and Media Law. https://artandmedialaw.com/privacy-and-data-protection-in-streaming-law/?amp=1

Bloomberg Law. (2023, December 13). *California consumer privacy laws – CCPA & CPRA*. Bloomberg Law. https://pro.bloomberglaw.com/insights/privacy/california-consumer-privacy-laws/

Boatman, A. (2023, July 24). *Pre-employment screening: Your comprehensive guide [for 2023]*. AIHR. https://www.aihr.com/blog/pre-employment-screening/

Boland, M. & Hofstrand, D. (2021). *The role of the board of directors*. Ag Decision Maker. Iowa State University. https://www.extension.iastate.edu/agdm/wholefarm/html/c5-71.html

Bondale, K. (2019, October 22). *12 real-life examples of project risk management strategies*. The Digital Project Manager. https://thedigitalprojectmanager.com/projects/risk-management/project-risk-management-strategies/

Bryce, I. (2022, December 5). *What is contract management?* Gatekeeperhq. https://www.gatekeeperhq.com/blog/what-is-contract-management

Business insurance claims: How to file claims and get paid out faster. (2024, June 6). FreshBooks. https://www.freshbooks.com/hub/insurance/business-insurance-claims

Chatterton, C. (2023, August 17). *The ultimate guide to risk prioritization*. Hyperproof. https://hyperproof.io/resource/the-ultimate-guide-to-risk-prioritization/

Chumak, A. (2023, December 1). *Data protection in the financial services industry*. InCountry. https://incountry.com/blog/data-protection-in-the-financial-services-industry/

Consumer data. (n.d.). NIQ. https://nielseniq.com/global/en/info/consumer-data/

Coursera Staff. (2023, July 20). *9 cybersecurity best practices for businesses in 2023.* Coursera. https://www.coursera.org/articles/cybersecurity-best-practices

Curwen, L. (2021, August 3). *The collapse of Enron and the dark side of business.* BBC News. https://www.bbc.co.uk/news/business-58026162

Datasniper. (2024). *From planning to reporting: Exploring the phases of the audit process.* Datasnipper. https://www.datasnipper.com/resources/phases-of-the-audit-process

DLA Piper. (2023, January 29). *Law in the United States - DLA Piper Global data protection laws of the world.* Dlapiperdataprotection. https://www.dlapiperdataprotection.com/index.html?t=law&c=US

Eby, K. (2023, March 23). *The essentials of business risk mitigation.* Smartsheet. https://www.smartsheet.com/content/risk-mitigation

Euronext. (2024). *8 steps to develop a strong compliance strategy (and why you should).* Corporateservices.euronext. https://www.corporateservices.euronext.com/blog/compliance/strategy

Evans, B. "21 Hand-Picked Knowledge Quotes To Inspire You." Tettra. Last modified May 8, 2023. https://tettra.com/article/knowledge-quotes/.

Expert Panel. (2024, January 30). *Council post: 20 cybersecurity strategies businesses can implement today.* Forbes. https://www.forbes.com/sites/forbesfinancecouncil/2024/01/30/20-cybersecurity-strategies-businesses-can-implement-today/

Farnham, K. (2021). *9 strategic risk examples and how to successfully tackle them.* Diligent. https://www.diligent.com/resources/blog/strategic-risk-examples

Federal Trade Commission. (2018, October 31). *Financial privacy.* Federal Trade Commission. https://www.ftc.gov/news-events/topics/protecting-consumer-privacy-security/financial-privacy

Federal Trade Commission. (2021, February). *Data breach response: A guide for business.* Federal Trade Commission. https://www.ftc.gov/business-guidance/resources/data-breach-response-guide-business

Free Law. (2024, June 19). *Data protection laws in India: current scenario and future prospects.* Free Law: Get Free Headnotes & Judgments; Free Law. https://www.freelaw.in/legalarticles/Data-Protection-Laws-in-India-Current-Scenario-and-Future-Prospects-

Gargaro, D. (2021, May 7). *What is general liability insurance?* Business.com. https://www.business.com/insurance/general-liability/

Goh, F. (2020). *10 companies that failed to innovate, resulting in business failure.* Collective Campus. https://www.collectivecampus.io/blog/10-companies-that-were-too-slow-to-respond-to-change

Gupta, A. (2023, August 21). *Digital personal data protection act, 2023 – an overview - KPMG India.* KPMG. https://kpmg.com/in/en/home/insights/2023/08/digital-personal-data-protection-act-2023-overview.html

HealthIT. (2018). *Health information privacy law and policy.* HealthIT. https://www.healthit.gov/topic/health-information-privacy-law-and-policy

Herold, R. (2018, September 3). *12 reasons why data privacy protection brings business value.* CPO Magazine. https://www.cpomagazine.com/blogs/privacy-intelligence/12-reasons-why-data-privacy-protection-brings-business-value

Hosken, M. (2023, August 4). *How to write a privacy policy in 10 easy steps.* Website-Policies. https://www.websitepolicies.com/blog/how-to-write-a-privacy-policy

Information Commissioner's Office. (2023, August 7). *Your beginner's guide to data protection.* ICO. https://ico.org.uk/for-organisations/advice-for-small-organisations/your-beginner-s-guide-to-data-protection/

Insurance Advisor Team. (2024, January 25). *Professional liability insurance: Coverage, types, importance and cost.* InsuranceAdvisor.com. https://www.insuranceadvisor.com/resources/professional-liability-insurance

Islam, R. (2022, October 31). *Council post: how to respond to a business data breach in under 60 minutes.* Forbes. https://www.forbes.com/sites/forbestechcouncil/2022/10/31/how-to-respond-to-a-business-data-breach-in-under-60-minutes/

Janeczko, B. (2020, August 25). *Covering all the bases: How to set the legal framework for your new business.* Entrepreneur. https://www.entrepreneur.com/growing-a-business/covering-all-the-bases-how-to-set-the-legal-framework-for/354635

Katz, E. (2021, January 10). *6 steps to developing a data breach response plan.* Spectral. https://spectralops.io/blog/6-steps-data-breach-response-plan/

Kazlauskas, P. (2023, August 14). *Understanding the importance of crisis management teams.* Threshold Security. https://thresholdsecurity.com/understanding-the-importance-of-crisis-management-teams/

Keener, M. (2020, April 16). *Customer data: everything you need to know.* Insightly. https://www.insightly.com/blog/customer-data-types/

Kenton, W. (2023, November 3). *Business risk.* Investopedia. https://www.investopedia.com/terms/b/businessrisk.asp

Kilroy, A. (2023, January 10). *Insurance brokers: Do you really need one?* Forbes Advisor. https://www.forbes.com/advisor/insurance/do-you-need-insurance-broker/

Korolov, M. (2020, July 7). *California consumer privacy act (CCPA): What you need to know to be compliant.* CSO Online. https://www.csoonline.com/article/565923/california-consumer-privacy-act-what-you-need-to-know-to-be-compliant.html

Lam, J. (2024, January 24). *What is professional liability insurance?* Forbes. https://www.forbes.com/advisor/business-insurance/professional-liability-insurance/

Leggett, T. (2021, July 30). *Amazon hit with $886m fine for alleged data law breach.* BBC News. https://www.bbc.com/news/business-58024116

Leonard, K. (2021, November 3). *What is directors & officers (D&O) insurance?* Business.com. https://www.business.com/insurance/directors-officers/

LinkedIn Community. (2023). *How do you prioritize and rank risks based on their likelihood and impact?* LinkedIn. https://www.linkedin.com/advice/1/how-do-you-prioritize-rank-risks-based-likelihood-1f

Lucidchart. (2018, June 11). *A complete guide to the risk assessment process.* Lucidchart. https://www.lucidchart.com/blog/risk-assessment-process

Metzger, J. (2023, November 23). *8 common types of business insurance.* Forbes. https://www.forbes.com/advisor/business-insurance/types-of-business-insurance/

MoneyControl News. (2023, August 23). *RBI introduces digital personal data protection (DPDP) Act, 2023 for regulated entities: Key points.* Moneycontrol. https://www.moneycontrol.com/news/business/rbi-introduces-digital-personal-data-protection-dpdp-act-2023-for-regulated-entities-key-points-11213691.html

Mousavi, B. (2022, October 12). *Business insurance claims process: Everything you need to know.* Coverwallet. https://blog.coverwallet.com/claim-process-insurance

National Law Review. (2023, September 4). *Federal Trade Commission enforcement actions focus on health information privacy.* The National Law Review. https://www.natlawreview.com/article/federal-trade-commission-enforcement-actions-focus-health-information-privacy

NCSL. (2020, November 17). *Data security laws | State government data breach laws.* Ncsl.org. https://www.ncsl.org/technology-and-communication/data-security-laws

Nichols, A. (2022, December 16). *Cybersecurity basics: What are firewalls?* Cisco. https://www.cisco.com/c/en/us/products/security/firewalls/what-is-a-firewall.html

Nolan, J. (2021, April 12). *Why your business needs professional liability insurance.* Fitsmallbusiness.com. https://fitsmallbusiness.com/professional-liability-insurance/

Phillips, C. (2022, December 12). *6 important things to include in a data breach response plan.* Netwrix Blog. https://blog.netwrix.com/2022/12/12/6-important-things-to-include-in-a-data-breach-response-plan/

Pinsent Masons. (2023, December 6). *Cyber security basics: Why every business needs a plan.* Pinsent Masons. https://www.pinsentmasons.com/out-law/guides/cyber-security-basics

Roberts, B. (2022, September 21). *The most notorious business lawsuits of all time.* Investopedia. https://www.investopedia.com/articles/investing/030216/most-notorious-business-lawsuits-all-time.asp

Samaha, S. (2023, July 31). *The ultimate guide to project risk management.* ProjectManager. https://www.projectmanager.com/blog/ultimate-guide-to-project-risk-management

Schroeder, T. (2021, October 12). *What is pre-employment screening?* Paycor. https://www.paycor.com/resource-center/articles/pre-employment-screening/

Scully, J. (2023, July 28). *Risk prioritization: What you need to know.* Reciprocity. https://reciprocity.com/risk-prioritization-guide/

Securities and Exchange Commission. (2022). *The importance of good corporate governance.* https://www.sec.gov.ph/importance-of-good-corporate-governance/

Shin, K. (2022, January 5). *The importance of firewalls in network security.* Security Magazine. https://www.securitymagazine.com/articles/96890-the-importance-of-firewalls-in-network-security

Silva, M. (2021, August 3). *Health information privacy law and policy.* HealthIT.gov. https://www.healthit.gov/topic/health-information-privacy-law-and-policy

Smartsheet. (2024). *What is the project life cycle?* Smartsheet. https://www.smartsheet.com/content/project-lifecycle

Sow, P. (2022, October 11). *The importance of risk management planning.* Airswift. https://www.airswift.com/blog/the-importance-of-risk-management-planning

Stanwick, P. & Stanwick, S. (2013). *Understanding business ethics.* SAGE.

Stewart, H. (2022, September 13). *Financial privacy laws: How they're changing in 2022.* Metomic. https://metomic.io/blog/financial-privacy-laws-how-theyre-changing-in-2022

Stobierski, T. (2020, October 21). *Types of risk: different types of risk & how to manage them.* Harvard Business School Online. https://online.hbs.edu/blog/post/types-of-risk

Suryadi, S. (2021, August 26). *The 5 best incident management solutions for your business.* Vantage Circle. https://blog.vantagecircle.com/incident-management-solutions

TechTarget Contributor. (2023, April 28). *What is a digital risk management plan? Definition from TechTarget.* SearchCIO. https://www.techtarget.com/searchcio/definition/digital-risk-management-plan

Tuhus-Dubrow, R. (2023, March 31). *The death and life of great American newspapers.* The Nation. https://www.thenation.com/article/archive/death-and-life-great-american-newspapers/

Vane, T. (2022, December 6). *Risk management plan.* Business Expert. https://www.business-expert.co.uk/your-risk-management-plan

"What Happened to Grooveshark, the Music Streaming Service?" Failory: 90% of Startups Fail — Learn How Not To. Last modified 2024. https://www.failory.com/cemetery/grooveshark

Wong, J. (2023, April 5). *What is the GDPR? The summary guide to GDPR compliance in the UK.* IT Governance Blog En. https://www.itgovernance.co.uk/blog/what-is-gdpr-the-summary-guide-to-gdpr-compliance-in-the-uk

Zabelina, D. (2022, November 28). *How to make a data breach response plan: Examples & best practices.* SE Ranking Blog. https://seranking.com/blog/data-breach-response-plan/

Zacks Investment Research. (2023). *The importance of cash flow management.* Zacks. https://www.zacks.com/stock/news/112684/the-importance-of-cash-flow-management